City Breaks
in
Madrid, Barcelona
Seville & Granada
– a new look

REG BUTLER

In Association with

THOMSON HOLIDAYS

SETTLE PRESS

Text © 1996 Reg Butler

First published by Settle Press
10 Boyne Terrace Mews
London W11 3LR

ISBN (Paperback) 1 872876 46 3

Printed by Villiers Publications
19 Sylvan Avenue
London N3 2LE

Foreword

The world spotlight focussed on Spain throughout 1992, when the principal Spanish cities commemorated the fifth centenary of the Columbus voyage to the New World.

Since then, CityBreak visitors have enjoyed the huge expansion in the sightseeing potential especially of Madrid, Barcelona, Granada and Seville. These great cities have more to offer than ever before - spruced-up monuments, refurbished museums, new concert halls, improved facilities.

For this book Reg Butler travelled to each city, to interview the experts in charge of tourism programmes. He also worked closely with our resident Thomson representatives, who have year-round experience of helping visitors enjoy what each city can offer. All information has been up-dated for this 1996 edition, though telephone numbers, prices and opening times are always liable to change.

As Britain's leading short breaks specialist, we recognise the need for detailed guidance for CityBreak travellers. But much more is required than just a listing of museums. For a few days, the CityBreak visitor wants to experience the local lifestyle.

We're sure you'll find this book invaluable in planning how to make best personal use of your time.

Pocket guidebooks in the 'City Breaks' series now cover Vienna, Salzburg, Budapest and Prague; Paris; Amsterdam; Rome, Florence and Venice; Brussels and Bruges; Dublin; New York.

THOMSON CITYBREAKS

Contents

4. SEVILLE

5. GRANADA 94

6. FURTHER INFORMATION

Maps

Chapter One

Spain beyond the beaches

1.1 'Discovery' is still the theme

In 1992, world attention focussed on the 'different' Spain beyond the beaches. Commemorating the 5th centenary of the discovery of the New World in October 1492 became the "umbrella event" which helped to tip international votes in favour of Barcelona for the Olympics, Seville for Expo '92, and Madrid as the Cultural Capital of Europe.

Global TV exposure revealed Spain as a land with rich potential for cultural sightseeing and world-class entertainment, and not just a venue for budget-priced beach holidays amd cheap wine.

Typically, a spokesman for Andalusia, which includes Costa del Sol, said: "We wanted to develop a more balanced tourism product, putting the emphasis on the interior, not just on the coast. We wanted to offer the idea of artistic and sightseeing attractions, in which Andalusia is rich. Seville, Cordoba and Granada offer one of Spain's best groups of quality monuments."

With the world spotlight on Seville, there were constant reminders that the city is among the most beautiful in Spain, with a central area where Columbus could still discover many familiar landmarks.

In preparation for the big show, Seville was spruced up with better air, road and rail links, a spanking-new Maestranza Opera House, and a refurbished riverside promenade. With doubled hotel capacity, Seville is now much better equipped to host visitors.

Seville will always remain the highlight of travel-poster Spain: orange blossom, fiestas, flamenco and monuments from the Golden Age when the city had a monopoly of trade with the Americas. Even if you cannot visit Seville during the big fiestas, the city is certainly worth visiting any time you have a weekend to spare.

INTRODUCTION

Granada likewise has played a big part in Spanish history. January 1492 saw the surrender of Granada by the Moorish King Boabdil to the conquering Christian armies of Isabella and Ferdinand. The triumphant Spanish monarchs moved into the Alhambra fortress palace – an Arabian-nights' fantasy – established a temporary Cathedral in a mosque and signed a contract with Columbus to sponsor his voyage of discovery. The enchantment of the Alhambra has survived the passage of 500 years as a supreme monument of Muslim art and architecture.

From 1561 the Spanish monarchs moved their court to the more central location of Madrid, and built up the original dusty fortress town into a European capital in grandest style.

Especially during the 17th century, Spain's great artists and writers flocked to the royal court. Many of Madrid's finest buildings date from the following century.

Madrid has always enjoyed very high standing on the European art-lovers' circuit. Most famous is the Prado art gallery, which rates among Europe's top three: rich and comprehensive, with the world's finest collection of paintings by Goya, Velázquez and El Greco.

In the same area the Palace of Villahermosa has been converted to house the Thyssen-Bornemisza art collection from Lugano – the second most important private collection in the world, after that of Britain's royal family.

Further down the Paseo del Prado is the Queen Sofia Art Centre, opened in 1986, with 12,500 square metres of exhibition galleries – about three times the space of London's Tate Gallery. Quite apart from its permanent collection – now expanding through loans, legacies and purchases – this Contemporary Art Center can easily handle up to five temporary exhibitions simultaneously. Here, too, Picasso's awesome *Guernica* is displayed.

Even a commercial activity like building a new Trade Fair and Conference Center can have a cultural gloss. A new Exhibition Park was opened in 1991 two miles from the airport, with direct access to the city centre.

In the adjoining City Park – Campo de las Naciones – the Municipality sponsored ten major works of modern sculpture. On a permanent basis, the aim is to establish Madrid as the world capital of open-air sculpture, in which the city is already rich.

During 1992 Barcelona – Spain's second city – became the world capital of sport. At the fourth attempt, Barcelona's bid to host the Olympics was successful, and

INTRODUCTION

July 1992 saw Barcelona on a billion TV screens around the world, with an audience of 3,500 million.

Barcelona is a city with a long sporting tradition, and is famed throughout Europe as home to one of the world's most famous football clubs. Barcelona boasts more than 1,300 sports centres and 1,200 public and private clubs.

As a dynamic industrial and commercial centre, Barcelona is mainly considered as a business travel destination, and a venue for trade fairs and conferences.

But there's much more to Barcelona than business and sport. The Catalonian capital offers rich sightseeing and cultural attractions which make it an ideal citybreak destination, anything from three days to a week.

Most holidaymakers to Costa Brava or Costa Dorada take a whole-day sightseeing excursion to Barcelona. They stroll along the world-famous Ramblas, explore the Gothic quarter around the ancient Cathedral, and visit the Columbus Column and a neighbouring replica of the *Santa Maria*. Coach tours include a photo-stop for the extraordinary architecture of the unfinished church, the Sagrada Familia, which became the life's work of the way-out Catalan architect, Gaudí.

Anyone staying longer in Barcelona can explore the Gaudí genius in more detail. As a pioneer of the 'Modernist' movement – the Catalan equivalent of Art Nouveau or Art Deko – Gaudí left his fantastic imprint on a dozen major buildings and park areas.

Barcelona's museums are rich in Catalonian culture, which is quite separate from the rest of Spain. The city also became a leader in 20th-century avant-garde art.

Picasso spent his boyhood years in Barcelona. The local Picasso Museum – housed in two noble palaces – contains a spread of his life's work: earliest paintings, Blue Period, and a series from his later productions including ceramics.

Another ultra-modern artist – Joan Miró – established his own Foundation on Montjuïc mountain, close to the main Olympic Stadium and the 'Olympic Ring' of sport venues. Also on Monjuïc is the Museum of Catalonian Art, housed in a Palace reconstructed by the same Italian architect who master-minded the Musée d'Orsay in Paris.

There's no need to wait until another major sporting event to enjoy Barcelona. Likewise Seville, Granada and Madrid are cities for any time you can spare a long weekend. These Citybreak destinations will continue to delight in the years to come. Now's the time to discover Spain beyond the beaches!

1.2 Which season?

Springtime is a splendid season for Seville or Granada, before the summertime heat is switched on. In Andalusia springtime comes early. Almond blossom begins in January and lasts into early February. By mid-February, wild flowers are in full bloom: asphodel, anemones, jonquil, iris, bluebells, and entire hedges of geranium. Peach blossom is opening, and swallows build nests. In March, roses bloom in temperatures like an English June, but cool nights.

Madrid: The best months are March-April and October-November. Springtime in the heart of Spain is a period of sparkling blue skies, averaging 7 hours' sunshine daily and noon temperatures of 60°. Nights are chilly. November, Madrid has Europe's best sunshine record, 6 hours daily.

Madrid swelters in high summer, but air conditioning helps make life tolerable. It's then best to go ethnic with a siesta to avoid the grilling afternoon heat.

Barcelona: Late April, May and early June have a charm of their own, and the weather is glorious. In late September and October, the sea is at its warmest after months of sunshine, and the skies are still blue.

Temperatures – average daily maximum (°F)

	Jan	Feb	Mar	Apr	May	Jun	Jul	Aug	Sep	Oct	Nov	Dec
Madrid	49	52	59	65	70	81	88	86	77	66	56	49
Barcelona	56	58	61	65	70	77	83	83	77	70	61	56
Seville or Granada	59	63	69	74	79	90	95	97	90	79	68	61
London, for comparison	43	45	49	54	60	68	72	73	65	58	52	47

Monthly rainfall – inches

	Jan	Feb	Mar	Apr	May	Jun	Jul	Aug	Sep	Oct	Nov	Dec
Madrid	1.5	1.3	1.7	1.9	1.9	1.0	0.4	0.4	1.2	2.0	1.9	1.9
Barcelona	1.2	1.5	1.9	1.7	2.1	1.4	1.0	1.9	3.0	3.4	2.0	1.8

Chapter Two

Madrid

2.1 A capital city break

From the small central town where Philip 11 established his court in 1561, Madrid has thrived across four centuries as the Spanish capital. The city growth can neatly be divided into four or five main periods.

The heart of the city grew around an original 9th-century Moorish fortress, followed by Christian re-occupation in 11th and 12th centuries. But even for the next few hundred years, as part of the Kingdom of Castile, Madrid was little more than a collection of narrow streets with a mixed Christian, Moslem and Jewish population.

Only a very few traces of Moorish and Christian walls are still left from that medieval Madrid. The most visible remnant is located in the Plaza de la Villa, where the pre-15th-century Tower of los Lujanes, one of the city's oldest buildings, faces the Town Hall. *See map, fig. 36.*

From the 15th century Madrid began to find royal favour. Then Charles V gave the city a series of special privileges. In 1528 Philip 1 was sworn in as heir to the throne in the Madrid monastery of St. Jerome, and from then on Madrid never looked back. Some of the original pattern of narrow, twisting streets still survives in the central area around Plaza Mayor. *See map, fig. 31.*

During the reign of Philip II (1556-1598) the city boomed through the presence of the court in the old Alcazar while the major building project of El Escorial Monastery was under way. In 1607 Madrid became Spain's permanent capital and grew rapidly under the Habsburg rule of the House of Austria. Development focussed around the Plaza Mayor, completed during the reign of Philip III. The great sightseeing highlights of Madrid date especially from this period.

A major change of style came when Spanish Habsburg rule was replaced from 1700 by the House of Bourbon, in the person of Philip V.

With the Bourbons came the fashionable architecture of France and Italy. Following on a big fire in 1734 which destroyed the existing palace, urban renewal was better

11

planned with drains, paved roads and street lighting. Science and culture flourished with the establishment of Royal Academies of Language, History and Medicine. From this period came the existing Royal Palace, the foundation of the Botanical Gardens, and construction of what became the Prado Museum, though originally intended as a Natural Science Museum.

From early 19th century came a further wave of building, sometimes described as Romantic or Isabelline architecture. Among the best examples is the Palace of Linares, which occupies a corner of Cibeles Square (see map, fig. 6). This was the period of 'modern' Madrid with proliferation of theatres, banks, restaurants, cafes and the arrival of the railway. Great mansions were built in select districts like Salamanca – owned not just by the nobility, but also by families made rich from industry and trade.

Finally we have contemporary Madrid that has arisen during the past 50 years since the end of the Civil War. Mainly a 19th-century city, Madrid now has entire boulevards of modern apartments and a completely 20th-century University, rebuilt since wartime destruction. The first skyscrapers appeared, huge office blocks line the principal avenues, and dramatic modern architecture is opening up entire new areas of Madrid, especially towards the northern suburbs.

The process continues, with great vigour. As a vibrant modern capital, Madrid certainly does not live in the past, even though the central areas are so packed with sightseeing interest.

The marriage between past and present was highlighted during 1992, when Madrid served its year as Cultural Capital of Europe. That was linked with a huge civic and national-budget programme to improve all facilities and infrastructure, including transport.

Serious money was involved. The municipality, the regional government and a long list of commercial sponsors spent £120 million on the event.

In general, visitors know Madrid for their chosen hotel, the Prado Museum, and some restaurants and bars. Who knows anything about Madrid outside that? So the aim was to unveil much more of the Madrid of the last 400 years, and to reveal lesser-known areas of Madrid's culture.

For instance, plans were made to introduce Zarzuela to a wider international audience. Zarzuela is a light-hearted 19th-century form of comic opera very typical of Madrid, derived from the city streets and its characters. It occupies a very special corner of music which is unfamiliar to most non-Spaniards.

Several other 1992 projects aimed to make Madrid better known even to its own citizens. The City Museum – located next to the National Auditorium in Principe de Vergara Avenue – offers a complete picture of the history of Madrid. An old slaughterhouse re-lives as the Arganzuela Cultural Complex, headquarters of several artistic associations including the national ballet.

The beautiful and historic Linares Palace on Cibeles Square now houses the Museum of America, a cultural centre for relations between Spain and Latin America. Lope de Vega's house, where he lived for 25 years, has become a Centre for Studies on the Golden Age.

For art lovers, Madrid is now much more than the city of the Prado. Since October 1992, one of the world's richest private art collections – the Thyssen-Bornemisza collection – has moved from Lugano in Switzerland to a prestigious new home in the Palace of Villahermosa, just across the avenue from the Prado. *See map, fig. 17.*

Simultaneously, what is regarded as the greatest painting of the 20th century – Picasso's *Guernica* – has been moved further down the avenue to the Reina Sofia Art Centre. That magnificent centre for 20th-century art is itself converted from a remarkable 18th-century building which originally was designed as the Madrid General Hospital! *See map, fig. 27.* In Madrid, the past and the present live most happily together.

2.2 – Arrival & Public Transport

From Madrid-Barajas airport, yellow buses every 20 minutes cover the 10-mile, 30-minute drive to an underground terminal at Plaza de Colón – Columbus Square – in the city centre for 360 ptas including luggage. From there you can take a low-cost cab ride to any downtown hotel. A taxi to or from the airport costs around 3,400 ptas.

Madrid's public transport system is cheap and efficient. Spend a few minutes to learn layout of the Metro system which operates from 6 a.m. till 1.30 a.m. Any station will give you a free map of the network which comprises 11 lines, numbered 1 to 10, plus R. Single tickets cost 130 ptas, valid for travel any distance including any interchange. A ticket valid for 10 journeys costs 645 ptas. You buy them at the station.

The handiest line is Number 2, which links many of the principal sights:

Opera – Royal Palace
Sol – central to the system, at Puerto del Sol, within easy reach of Plaza Mayor and 'old' Madrid
Sevilla – equally handy for Puerto del Sol
Banco de España – for Plaza de Cibeles, and a short walk to Prado Museum
Retiro – for Retiro Park

MADRID

Buses run from 6 a.m. till midnight, single ticket 130 ptas, or 10 rides for 645 ptas. A half-hourly or hourly service operates in the small hours from Plaza de Cibeles and Puerta del Sol.

Taxis start from 125 ptas at flag-down, or higher on the night tariff from 11 p.m. A 10% tip is customary. If it's a longish journey across town, ask the driver the approximate cost before entering the taxi. Varied supplements are added for Sundays and public holidays, for rides to and from the airport, and for suitcases.

2.3 Get your bearings

Madrid's centre is compact, and while it has cheapish taxis, walking is more fun. Wandering around the rabbit-warren of the oldest areas of Madrid, it's easy to get lost. But that's all part of the charm, helping you get the feel of the past. Cobbled streets lead into peaceful little squares and thence up flights of steps to another view.

The easiest way to get your bearings is to open up a map of Central Madrid, and fix where the main highlights are located.

Puerta del Sol

The undisputed centre of Spain is Puerta del Sol, a pedestrianized Picadilly Circus from which all distances in Spain are measured. Here's a good cross-section of Madrid street-life, the liveliest area in town. It's a major subway and bus-line interchange point, brimming with people en route to the popular-price shopping streets around, including the big department stores. There are street musicians, hawkers, drifters, newspaper vendors, tourists. Surrounding streets are crammed with smaller shops, bars and restaurants. Much photographed is the popular symbol of Madrid – the statue of a Bear and a Strawberry Tree. *See map, fig. 29.*

Only two minutes away, along Calle Mayor, brings you into Plaza Mayor; or, in the opposite direction along Calle de San Jerónimo, within 6 or 7 minutes you can arrive at the Prado. Any of the streets going north – Preciados, Carmen or Montera – bring you into Gran Vía, if you ever make it past all the shops. Eastwards along Calle de Alcalá, past the Central Bank, takes you to Plaza de la Cibeles with its enormous fountains.

Calle Mayor

Here's the most historic road of Madrid, running from Puerta del Sol to the new Cathedral of La Almudena, inaugurated in 1992. En route is the Plaza Mayor, a delightful covered market called Mercado de San Miguel, and the superb Plaza

de la Villa – Town Hall Square. In the Tower of los Lujanes, King Francis 1 of France was imprisoned in 1525. *See
map, fig. 36.*

Plaza de Oriente
If you're walking the route along Calle Mayor, turn right at
the end by the new Cathedral, along Calle de Bailen to the
Royal Palace. Next is the small park called Plaza de Oriente
with lined-up statues of Visigoth monarchs and an equestrian
Philip 1V in the middle, patterned on a famed portrait by
Velázquez.

Facing the Palace is the Royal Theatre, restored to its
original use of Opera House in time for 1992. Behind the
Opera House is Opera metro station. But you're then also
fairly close to the Convent of Descalzas Reales *(see map,
fig. 30),* which is of major art-museum interest. Alterna-
tively, from Plaza de Oriente, two blocks north along Calle
de Bailen brings you up to Plaza de España.

Plaza de España and Gran Vía
Direct by public transport, take the metro to Pl. de España
(see map, fig. 44). This green park oasis among the swirling
traffic features a delightful Cervantes monument with Don
Quixote and his faithful Sancho Panza. Instead of windmills,
twin skyscrapers dominate the Plaza. Here is 20th-century
Madrid, with Gran Vía built entirely from 1910 onwards in
the glitter style of Broadway: shops, offices, bars, restaurants
and night-spots – over a mile downhill to Alcala.

Paseo del Prado
At the end of Calle de Alcalá is Plaza de la Cibeles, one of
Madrid's major landmarks and crossroads. The goddess Sybil
sits in a two lion-power chariot, surrounded by a wedding-
cake Post Office, the newly-renovated Linares Palace, the
Bank of Spain and the Palace of Buenavista. *See map, fig. 8.*

Due south runs Paseo del Prado, ranking as the world's
greatest avenue of art. At the Plaza Canovas del Castillo,
with its Neptune Fountain, are located the luxury-grade
Palace and Ritz hotels. The Palace of Villahermosa has been
restored *(see map, fig. 17),* to house the Thyssen-Bornemisza
art collection for at least the next decade.

Opposite is the Prado Museum and its various annexes
including the Cason del Buen Retiro. An adjoining gateway
is entrance to Retiro Park. Otherwise, continuing south
there's a 'Parnassus' area where painters and writers have
lived since early 17th century, including Cervantes and Lope
de Vega – and thence to the Botanical Gardens and the
Queen Sofia Art Centre. Opposite is Atocha's brilliant new
railway station, named after a sanctuary called the Virgen de
Atocha. Calle de Atocha leads directly back to Plaza Mayor.

MADRID

1 – Plaza de Colón – Airport Bus Terminal; City Cultural Centre; Columbus Monument and Gardens of the Discovery
2 – National Library and Archaeological Museum
3 – Wax Museum
4 – Law Courts
5 – Alcalá Gate, Plaza Independencia
6 – Linares Palace
7 – Palace of Buenavista
8 – Cibeles Fountain
9 – General Post Office
10 – Bank of Spain
11 – Naval Museum
12 – Decorative Arts Museum
13 – Zarzuela Theatre
14 – Congress of Deputies
15 – Stock Exchange
16 – Obelisk of 2nd May, and Unknown Soldier memorial
17 – Thyssen Museum
18 – Army Museum
19 – Museum of 19th-century Art
20 – Retiro Park
21 – Neptune Fountain
22 – Lope de Vega House
23 – Prado Museum
24 – Botanical Gardens
25 – Book Market
26 – National Ethnological Museum
27 – Queen Sofia Art Centre
28 – San Fernando Academy of Fine Arts
29 – Puerto del Sol; Bear statue
30 – Las Descalzas Reales Convent
31 – Plaza Mayor
32 – Foreign Office
33 – San Miguel market
34 – San Isidro Cathedral
35 – Rastro street market
36 – Plaza de la Villa; Town Hall; Lujanes Tower
37 – Royal Theatre
38 – Palace of Capitania General
39 – Almudena Cathedral
40 – Royal Palace
41 – Campo del Moro
42 – Plaza Oriente
43 – Palace of the Senate
44 – Plaza de España; Cervantes and Don Quixote
45 – Edificio España skyscraper
46 – Cerralbo Museum

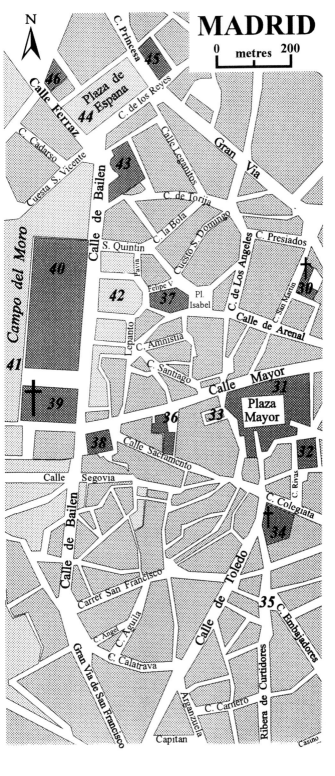

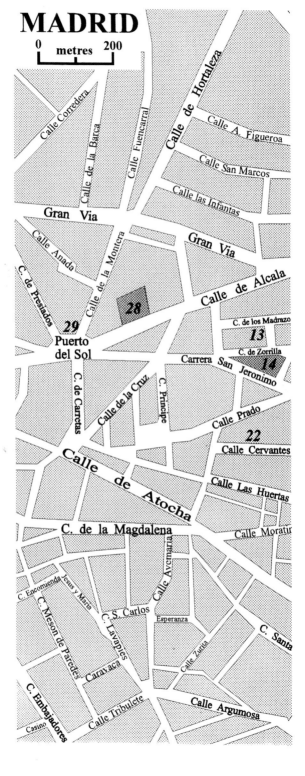

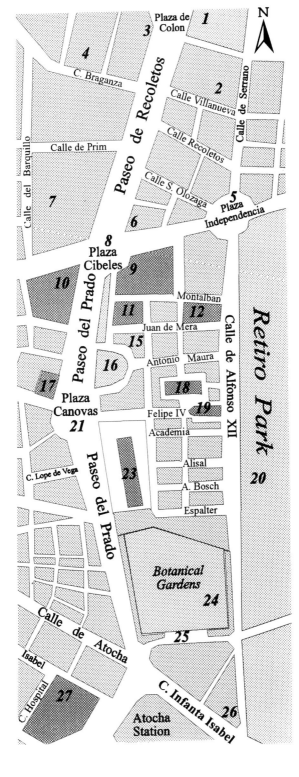

MADRID

Paseo de Recoletos

North from Plaza de la Cibeles is the broad boulevard Paseo de Recoletos which is lined with the most prestigious architecture of recent decades, dedicated mainly to banking and commerce. Plaza de Colón includes a 20th-century tribute to the Discoveries of Columbus, with fascinating macro-sculptures by Vaquero Turcios.

The main boulevard continues north as Paseo de la Castellana, towards the airport. Running parallel from Alcala Gate at the corner of Retiro Park is Calle Serrano, the very exclusive shopping street and up-market residential area.

2.4 Seeing basic Madrid

Give yourself a month, and you can see everything in Madrid. Otherwise, on a short city break, at least try to cover the essentials:

(1) Admire the Plaza Mayor and its splendid 16th-century arcaded buildings, and explore the surrounding side streets of 'old' Madrid. *See map, fig. 31.*
(2) Pay homage to Goya, Velázquez and El Greco at the Prado art gallery. *See map, fig. 23.*
(3) Make a special point to see the Thyssen-Bornemisza art collection in Villahermosa Palace. *See map, fig. 17.*
(4) Visit the Reina Sofia Art Centre close by for Picasso's *Guernica*. *See map, fig. 27.*
(5) Tour the Royal Palace for its sumptuous museum collections – everything from watches and clocks to furniture and paintings. *See map, fig. 40.*
(6) Take an excursion to Toledo, and see how damascene steel is made.
(7) Sunday morning, take Metro to La Latina and enjoy El Rastro – Europe's liveliest flea market. *See map, fig. 35.*
(8) Savour the Madrileño lifestyle by spending early evening on a tasca-crawl, trying different tapas at each bar.
(9) Sample a flamenco show, or the Madrid comic-opera diversion called zarzuela. *See map, fig. 13.*
(10) Visit El Escorial, the great monastery-palace built in 16th century.

El Prado Museum, Paseo del Prado   Tel: 420 28 36
Madrid's top sightseeing attraction is the art-lovers' paradise of the Prado *(fig. 23)*, ranking among the finest in Europe.

Best policy is to take the standard guided tour to find where the greatest paintings are located, and then return another day for leisurely browsing. The gallery contains over 100 rooms and houses Europe's most impressive collection

of Spanish, Italian and Flemish paintings. In Spanish school, the Prado is especially rich in Velázquez, El Greco and Goya (including his famed Clothed and Naked Majas). If time is short, take the lift to the first floor and concentrate on those three artists. Nowhere else in the world can offer a finer collection.
Open: Tue-Sat 9.30-17.00 hrs; Sun and holidays 9-14 hrs. Entrance: 800 ptas. Free on Wednesdays. Also free for under-21's from EEC countries. Metro: Banco de España or Atocha. Buses: 10, 14, 27, 34, 37, 45, M-6.

Casón del Buen Retiro, 28 Alfonso X11 Street
An annexe of the Prado *(see map, fig. 19)*, closer to Retiro Park. Half of this former 17th-century royal ballroom is devoted to 19th-century Spanish painting.   Tel: 420 26 28
Open: 9-19 hrs. Sundays 9-14 hrs. Closed Mon.
Entrance: 400 ptas, or use same ticket as for the Prado.

Villahermosa Palace, Paseo del Prado 8   Tel: 420 39 44
The early 19th-century Palacio de Villahermosa *(see map, fig. 17)* has been totally renovated to house the Thyssen-Bornemisza art collection. This is one of the world's greatest private collections, formed by the Thyssen dynasty who became wealthy through iron, steel and banking.
   The basic collection was established by Baron Heinrich Thyssen-Bornemisza (1875-1947) who began to acquire paintings by German masters of 15th and 16th centuries. He then concentrated on Flemish and Dutch Schools, and finally on Italian, Spanish and French. From 1937 the collection was exhibited at Villa Favorita in Lugano, Switzerland.
   His youngest son, Hans Heinrich, followed in father's footsteps, but prefered to buy modern masters – French Impressionists, German Expressionists, Cubists, Russian Avant-Garde, and American painters of 19th and 20th centuries.
   Besides paintings, the collection also includes valuable sculptures, jewelry, gold boxes, European silver, furniture, and stage designs for theatre and ballet.
   Out of this fabulous Aladdin's Cave, 787 paintings will be exhibited in the Villahermosa Palace at least until year 2002.
Open: Tue-Sun 10-19 hrs. Entrance: 600 ptas.

Reina Sofia Art Centre, Santa Isabel 52   Tel: 467 5062
CARS – Centro de Arte Reina Sofia – is one of world's biggest exhibition buildings for 20th-century art, rivalled only by the Pompidou Centre in Paris. Now fully operational, the Centre *(see map, fig. 27)* was originally designed in 18th century as the Madrid General Hospital. The architect was Italian-born Sabatini whom Charles III brought from Naples to work on the Royal Palace.

MADRID

The hospital continued to function until recent times. It was then decided to transform the vacant structure into a major centre for 20th-century art, based on an existing Contemporary Art collection which had been housed in a less ideal location.

The structure has been converted into an 'intelligent' high-technology art museum, with a central computer to control security, temperature and air conditioning. The stone structure of the 18th century has been totally preserved, but with very unusual glass towers for the external elevators. The lifts open up panoramic views as you ride to the top.

It's now a permanent gallery for some 3,000 works, including masterpieces by Picasso, Miró, Juan Gris, Calder, Ernst, Sutherland, etc. There's space for several temporary shows to be held simultaneously – Spanish and international.

Many visitors go specially to see *Guernica* - probably Picasso's most famous painting, based on bombing of that city during the Spanish Civil War. Also displayed are preliminary sketches for this masterpiece, which came to Spain in 1981, on the centenary of Picasso's birth. Formerly the painting was housed in the Museum of Modern Art, New York. The huge canvas was protected for years behind bullet-proof plate glass, for it's a work which continued to arouse very deep emotions.

The Queen Sofia gallery is one of the few which is open on Mondays, closed Tuesdays. It also keeps late hours – 10-21 hrs; Sun 10-14.30. Entrance: 400 ptas.
Metro: Atocha. Buses: 18, 59, 85, 86, Circular.

Palacio Real – Royal Palace

Bailén Street. *See map, fig. 40.*   Tel: 248 74 04
This magnificent Bourbon palace, built between 1737 and 1764, is among the largest and best preserved in Europe, with around 3000 rooms. The last monarch to live here was King Alfonso X111, exiled in 1931 when Spain became a Republic. Since 1950 it has functioned as a museum, with visits to the gorgeously-furnished royal apartments, and to the adjoining Armory.

The palace is still used for glittering State occasions since restoration of the monarchy, though King Juan Carlos – grandson of Alfonso XIII – lives in simple style outside town at the modest Zarzuela Palace, a former hunting lodge.

As a museum, the palace houses superb collections of porcelain, furniture, watches, clocks, fans, paintings and tapestries. Look also at the delightful mid-16th-century pharmacy, with herbs neatly pigeon-holed in drawers that reach to the ceiling.
Open: 9.30-17.45 hrs; Sunday & holidays 9.30-14.00 hrs. Closed Mon. Entrance: 400 ptas. Free on Wednesdays.
Metro: Opera, or Plaza de España. Buses: 3, 25, 33, 39.

Plaza Mayor

Only a few minutes' walk from Puerta del Sol brings you to the heart of 17th-century Madrid, little changed since the Plaza Mayor was used for burning of heretics, for tournaments and bull-fights and the canonisation of saints. Three Spanish kings were proclaimed here. Among the finest buildings are La Casa de la Panadería, the Bakers' Guild-house; and La Casa de la Carnicería, the Butchers' Guild-house. *See map, fig. 31.*

The Bakers' building has now been converted into a cultural centre, devoted mainly to research and studies into the history of Madrid. The central statue is Philip III, in whose reign the square was built, around 1616.

Antique stores within the Plaza arcades are filled with all the clutter of the centuries. Close by are ancient restaurants with specialities like roast suckling-pig. In cellar wine-taverns, waiters are dressed like bandits. But nobody feels robbed when pitchers of wine cost so little.

Las Descalzas Reales Convent, 3 Plaza Descalzas Reales
Very central – close to Puerta del Sol – this convent was founded by Phillip II's sister Joan of Austria, purpose-built to accommodate nuns from Europe's aristocratic and royal families. The foundress herself launched the collection of high-quality paintings, sculptures, relics and gold embroideries. The art treasures grew over the centuries, thanks to generous gifts from the nuns and their families. In 1987 the convent was designated 'European Museum of the Year'.
Open: Tue-Fri 10.30-12.30 & 16.00-17.15 hrs; Sun 11.00-13.30. Entrance: 650 ptas.   Tel: 542 00 59
Metro: Sol, Opera or Callao. Buses: 1, 2, 5, 20, 46, 52, 53, 74. *See map, fig. 30.*

2.5 Other sights in Madrid

Museums and Galleries

Archaeological Museum, 13 Calle Serrano Tel: 577 79 12
Collections from prehistory to Middle Ages. *See map, fig. 2.*
The highlight is a replica of the Altamira caves, discovered in 1868 near Santillana in northern Spain, with 20,000 year old paintings – the 'Sistine Chapel of Prehistoric Art'.
Open: Tue-Sat 9.30-20.30; Sun 9.30-14.30 hrs. Entrance: 400 ptas. Metro: Colón or Serrano. Buses: 1, 9, 19, 51, 74.

Army Museum, Méndez Nuñez 1   Tel: 522 06 28
Military history, uniforms and hardware. *See map, fig. 18.*
Open: Wed-Sun 10-14 hrs. Entrance free.
Metro: Banco de España. Buses: 15, 19, 27, 34, 37, 45.

MADRID

Bullfight Museum, Las Ventas bullring, Alcala 237
History of bullfighting, costumes etc. A behind-the-scenes
tour includes a stroll through the operating theatre.
Open: Mon-Fri 9.30-14.30 hrs. Entrance free. Metro:
Ventas. Buses: 12, 21, 38, 53, M-1, M-8. Tel: 725 18 57

Cerralbo Museum, 17 Calle Ventura Rodriguez
The palace home of a great art collector, displaying paintings, engravings, tapestries, armour, furniture, ceramics and
a library. *See map, fig. 46.*
Open: Tue-Sat 9.30-14.30; Sun 10-14 hrs.
Entrance: 400 ptas. Metro: Plaza España or Ventura Rodriguez. Buses: 1, 2, 44, 74, C, M-5, M-9. Tel: 247 36 46

Coach Museum (Museo de Carruajes), Virgen del Puerto
Tel: 248 74 04
A valuable collection of royal carriages, harnesses and sad-
dles from 16th-20th centuries. In Campo del Moro *(see map,
fig. 41)*. Check whether still closed for renovation.
Normally open: Winter 10.00-12.45 and 15.30-17.45 hrs;
Summer 10.00-12.45 and 16.00-17.45 hrs. Closed: Sundays,
and holiday afternoons. Entrance: 300-500 ptas. Metro:
Norte. Buses: 25, 33, 39, 41, 46, 75.

Lázaro Galdiano Museum, 122 Calle Serrano
Tel: 561 60 84
A former palace containing an important private art collec-
tion donated to the city of Madrid. Paintings, furniture,
carpets and an unusual 19th-century painted paper collection.
Open: Wed-Sun 10-14 hrs. Entrance free. Metro: Núñez de
Balboa or Av. de America. Buses: 9, 16, 19, 51, 89.

Lope de Vega's House, 11 Cervantes Street
Lope de Vega lived here from 1610 till his death in 1635. It
has now been converted into a Centre for Studies on the
Golden Age. Tel: 439 92 16
Metro: Antón Martín. Buses: 6, 26, 32, 57, M-9.

Municipal Museum, Fuencarral 78 Tel: 521 66 56
A complete round-up of Madrid's history, with a city scale
model of 1830.
Open: Tue-Fri 9.30-20.00 hrs; Sat-Sun 10-14 hrs. Entrance
420 ptas. Metro: Tribunal. Buses: 3, 7, 40, 149.

National Museum of Decorative Arts, Montalbán 12
Spanish popular arts, especially rich in ceramics from 15th
to 19th centuries.
Open: Tue-Fri 9.30-15 hrs; Sat-Sun 10-14 hrs. Entrance 400
ptas. Metro: Banco de España. *See map, fig. 12.* Buses: 14,
19, 27, 34, 37, 45. Tel: 521 3440

24

Naval Museum, Paseo del Prado 5   Tel: 379 52 99
Nautical history of the Spanish navy, and a library which
includes the navigational chart of Juan de la Cosa, the ship's
master who sailed with Columbus on his first two voyages.
His world map was the first to show the new continent.
Open: Tue-Sun 10.30-13.30 hrs. Entrance free.
Metro: Banco de España. *See map, fig. 11.* Buses: 10, 14,
27, 34, 37, 45.

Open-air Sculptures Museum, Paseo de la Castellan
Located below the Eduardo Dato fly-over, abstract Spanish
sculptures presented by the artists to the people of Madrid.
Open: year-round, 0-24 hrs. Entrance free. Metro: Núñez de
Balboa, or Rubén Darío. Buses: 14, 27, 45, 150.

Railway Museum, Paseo Delicias 61   Tel: 527 31 21
Something to keep the steam buffs happy, a museum in a
former station. Locomotives from the past, and all the ancillary collectables.
Open: Tue-Sun 10-15 hrs. Entrance: 400 ptas. Metro: Delicias. Buses: 6, 8, 19, 45, 47, 85, 86.

Romantic Museum, San Mateo 13   Tel: 448 10 71
A 19th-century collection in an 18th-century palace, display-
ing the aristocratic life-style during the reign of Isabella 11.
It includes paintings by Murillo, Goya and Zurbarán.
Open: Tue-Sat 9-14.45; Sun 10-14 hrs. Entrance: 400 ptas.
Metro: Alonso Martínez or Tribunal. Buses: 37, 40, 149.

Royal Tapestry Factory, 2 Calle Fuenterrabia
Tapestries, drawings and carpets from 18th and 19th centu-
ries, with demonstration of traditional manufacturing process.
Open: Mon-Fri 9-12.30 hrs. Entrance: 200 ptas.
Metro: Menéndez Pelayo. Buses: 10, 14, 26, 32, 37, C, M-
9. Located near Atocha Station.   Tel: 551 34 00

Sorolla Museum, 37 General Martínez Campos
The house in which the Spanish painter Joaquin Sorolla
(1863-1923) lived and worked from 1912. Several of his
most outstanding works are among the numerous paintings
donated by his widow.
Open: Tue-Sat 10-14 hrs; Sun 10-14. Entrance 400 ptas.
Metro: Rubén Darío or Iglesia. Buses: 5, 7, 16, 61, 40, M-
3.   Tel: 310 15 84

Wax Museum, Paseo de Recoletos 41   Tel: 308 08 25
Every capital city nowadays must have one! Here are 400
historic and world personalities.
Open: 10-14 & 16-20.30 hrs. Entrance: 500 ptas.
Metro: Colón. Buses: 5, 14, 27, 45, 53, 150.

MADRID
Parks and Gardens

Botanical Gardens – located next to the Prado, laid out in 1781 and now has over 30,000 plant species from all over the world. *See map, fig. 24.*
Open: 10-20 hrs. Metro: Atocha.

Retiro Park – occupies almost 300 acres, a favourite location for Madrid families out for a weekend stroll around the boating lake and through the rose garden. Occasional art exhibitions are held in the Crystal Palace and the Velázquez Palace. *See map, fig. 20.*

Campo del Moro – the formal garden of the Royal Palace. *See map, fig. 41.*

2.6 Take a trip

Even on a very short visit to Madrid, be sure to make time for Toledo and/or El Escorial. They're in opposite directions from Madrid, and each requires at least a full morning or afternoon. Numerous guided coach tours make the trips every day. On a full-day deal featuring both locations, tours are routed back through central Madrid with a 'free' lunch.

El Escorial

25 miles from Madrid, is often described by Spaniards as 'the eighth wonder of the world'. It's a fantastic mixture of palace, monastery, hospital and mausoleum, built over a 21-year period to celebrate victory in 1557 over the French. Out of the 4,000 rooms, most are still used – partly as a museum, but also as a monastery and seminary with 80 resident monks; and as a school teaching law and economics. El Escorial is open to visitors 10-13.30 and 15.30-18.30 hrs, Tue-Sun, entrance 500 ptas.

The austere granite-block building is set 3,500 feet up in a mountain setting. Built on orders of Philip II, El Escorial was furnished in very simple style. Suffering from gout, the king was carried around in a special gout chair which is still preserved.

Luxury was added by later kings. The art gallery is very rich, including paintings by Titian, Veronese, Tintoretto and several El Greco's. There's also a splendid marble Cellini sculpture of Christ.

In contrast to the simplicity of the rest of the building, the Pantheon of Kings is wildly elaborate. An access staircase lined with Spanish marble reaches the tombs of most monarchs and their wives since Charles V, spaced around the walls on a shelfing system. A few empty slots await.

Another Pantheon is in much more statuesque style, with monuments of Carrara marble for the tombs of selected near relatives of the royal family. Children up to age 7 were buried in a kind of marble wedding-cake.

The French-style gardens were laid out by the Bourbon monarchs.

Valley of the Fallen – Valle de los Caidos
Five miles north of El Escorial is Franco's monument to the civil war which raged from 1936 to 1939. A basilica is tunnelled into the mountain, where about 80,000 people are buried, including Franco himself. Building started in 1940, finished in 1959.

A visit is normally included on coach tours to El Escorial. The approach road goes up through pine woods to the basilica, where an enormous cross 500 ft high dominates the Valley. The entire tunnelled construction is longer than St. Peter's Rome. The individual human being is totally dwarfed in this grandiose monument.

Toledo

43 miles south of Madrid, Toledo is a perfectly-preserved medieval city, with walls rising dramatically from its defensive position above the River Tagus. The entire city has been declared a National Monument, and all sore-thumb building is totally prohibited.

There are fantastic views from across the loop of the River. The panorama up the granite hillside to the great gothic Cathedral is quite unchanged from the *View of Toledo* painted by El Greco, who lived here from 1577 to 1614.

The House of El Greco on Samuel Levi Street is furnished reputedly in 16th-century period style, but the interest is mainly in the important museum collection of his paintings and in some Velázquez sketches.

Very close is the synagogue of El Transito dating from 1366 and financed by Samuel Levi who was Treasurer to Peter I of Castile. The building is now a Sephardic Museum – a reminder that Toledo had a flourishing Jewish community until the expulsions of 1492.

One other synagogue has survived in the area, mainly through its conversion into the church of Santa María la Blanca. Building craftsmen of the day were Arab, so the synagogue-cum-church looks more like a mosque, except for a Renaissance style cross.

Pre-1492, the three religions were living together quite peacefully. Because of that tolerance, Toledo became one of Europe's most important cultural centres. Here was founded the first school of translators.

Bibles in Hebrew, Korans in Arabic, and the writings of Aristotle – they were all faithfully translated thanks to Arabic philosophers. All that academic work was ended by the Spanish Inquisition.

Toiling uphill to the Cathedral, you get endless medieval views of narrow Moorish-style streets and open courtyards. Shops are filled with damascene steel souvenirs, produced by craftsmen using the same methods of centuries ago, when a Toledo sword was Best Buy for medieval knights.

In total contract to the simplicity of the synagogues is the highly ornate cathedral, where sculpture often runs riot. There is magnificent stained glass, original from the 15th and 16th centuries. The main chapel in the centre of the cathedral is a complete sculpture museum, summarising the New Testament. The choir stalls are carved to represent scenes from the final capture of Granada in 1492.

El Greco came originally from Crete, hoping for work at El Escorial. But his style was not appreciated at Philip II's court, so he settled in Toledo – to that city's ultimate fame and benefit. Twentyseven of El Greco's masterpieces are displayed in the Cathedral Sacristy, along with Velázquez, Goya and Caravaggio. His most brilliant work 'The Burial of the Conde de Orgaz' is displayed in the Santo Tome church. Full circle, Toledo now prospers by continuing to look like an El Greco painting.

2.7 Sunday in Madrid

Religious Services
The **Cathedral of La Almudena** was inaugurated in 1992, after a final spurt to complete the building which started in 1883, to replace the former church which dated from 9th century. Location is next to the Royal Palace.
British Chapel, Núñez de Balboa 43. Metro: Velázquez.
Israeli Community, Balmes 3. Metro: Iglesia.
Church of England, Hermosilla 43. Metro: Velázquez.
English Mass, Blanca de Navarra 9. Metro: Alonso Martínez.

Museums & Galleries
Remember that most museums are open Sundays, at least for the morning sessions; but are closed Mondays.

Shops & Street Markets
In the Plaza Mayor there's a Sunday-morning stamp and coin market, where you can buy one-cent American coins for 25 pesetas.

Walk due south from Plaza Mayor to San Isidro Cathedral and fork left into the huge open-air Rastro street market, selling everything from cheap consumer goods to the most expensive antiques and paintings.

Haggling is normal. It's a great place to spend Sunday morning – don't miss it! Remember it's extremely crowded, so keep a tight hold on handbag or wallet. The handiest metro is La Latina, and then it's a downhill stroll all the way.

If you're still in shopping mood, take the subway to the large shopping centre called Madrid-2, at La Vaguada on the northern outskirts of Madrid (Metro: Barrio del Pilar). The unusual and striking design is by the famous Lanzarote architect, César Manrique. The centre is open all day Sunday with 350 shops, bars and restaurants.

Other Sunday events

When in Spain, do as the Spaniards do – go to a football match! Madrid's two largest football teams, Real Madrid and Atletico Madrid, normally play every Sunday afternoon during the football season.

Bullfights

From Easter till October is bullfight season, with a programme every Sunday afternoon and sometimes on Thursdays. During festive May, 16 bullfights are scheduled.

Seven stops by Metro Line 2 from Sol to Ventas, the Plaza de Toros on a bullfight afternoon is colourful travel-poster Spain. Even if you disapprove, a bullfight could be excused for the drama and traditional pageantry. Buy the cheapest seat, and you can always stalk out indignantly after the first bull!

2.8 Shopping

Madrid's main shopping areas have been mentioned in section 2.3 on 'Getting your Bearings'. Stores around Puerta del Sol, Gran Vía and Serrano should cover the full range of Spanish shopping. See the previous section 2.7 for Sunday shopping.

More specialised little shops with charming olde-worlde atmosphere are tucked around the Plaza Mayor area. Antique stores are clustered thickly along San Jerónimo and Calle del Prado, around El Rastro flea market (antique shops and galleries are open there weekdays as well as Sundays), and in the Puerta de Toledo Market (Metro Pta. de Toledo) where numerous master craftsmen are also gathered.

Art Galleries

Madrid's innumerable private-sector art galleries are open free from 11-14 hrs and 17-21 hrs every weekday. A complete listing of shows and museum galleries is published in *Arte y Exposiciones*, available at Tourism Offices, museums and galleries which are members of the Professional Association of Art Galleries.

Booklovers should visit the Booksellers' Row of Cuesta Claudio Moyano, alongside the Botanical Gardens. *See map, fig. 25.* Open daily, 10-18.30 hrs, including Sun. Metro: Atocha.

Toledo is the city for steel souvenirs of every possible type – knives, scissors, swords, cuff-links and suchlike. Prices and quality need watching carefully. Toledo craftsmen also produce damascene jewelry with gold and silver inlays often based on 8th-century Arab designs.

For a down-to-earth food market, visit the 19th-century covered **Mercado de San Miguel** on the next block to Plaza Mayor, for superb displays of fruit, veg and other victuals. Get a picture or two, with flash.

2.9 Eating Out in Madrid

To get the most enjoyment from a Madrid break, it's worth going Spanish with 2 o'clock lunch and 10 p.m. dinner.

Then you can sample the café and tavern life of Madrid. After a hard morning's sightseeing, it's pleasant to relax with a few sherries at a pavement or terrace café. Little saucers of snacks – *tapas* – help fight off hunger.

Then, early evening, get yourself into the Madrid lifestyle with a Spanish *tasca*-crawl. *Tasca* is a bar or winetavern, with great variety of snacks displayed along the counter. Between 7 p.m. and 10 all the central bars are thronged with local citizens – gossiping, drinking and eating the *tapas*. There are dozens of these bars in the Puerto del Sol area. A typical Madrid tapa is *patatas bravas* – cooked potatoes finished off under the grill, and eaten with a hot sauce.

Don't book even half board at Madrid hotels. Instead, break away from hotel 'international cuisine' and sample real Spanish food in characteristic local restaurants.

Among Madrid's 3,000 eating places, there is bewildering choice. If you want detailed guidance, ask at a Madrid Tourist Board information bureau for their excellent free booklet called "Madrid Gastronomy".

Otherwise, here's a short list which you may like to sample, including variety from the regional cuisines. Approximate price indications are:

£££ – £20+
££ – £10-£20
£ – under £10

Most restaurants offer adequate choice on their set menu deal, which can be a good moneysaver compared with ordering à la carte.

Alkalde, Jorge Juan 10   Tel: 576 33 59 ££
A bar and restaurant just off the fashionable Calle Serrano.
Basque cuisine. A speciality is Sopa de Centollo, a dream-
like cream soup made of crab.
Open: 13-16 & 20.30-24.00 hrs. Closed Sat nights and
Sundays in July/August.

Bajamar, Gran Vía 78   Tel: 248 48 18 £££
Galician seafood restaurant, considered among the best in
Madrid, but can be very expensive.
Open: 12-16 & 20-24 hrs.

Casa Botin, Cuchilleros 17   Tel: 366 42 17 ££
Founded in 1725, offers splendid atmosphere in its setting
just below Plaza Mayor. Renowned for its bull-fighting
guests, Hemingway associations, and roast suckling pig
cooked in the restaurant's original 267-year-old oven.
Reservations essential, with two sittings: 20 and 22 hrs. Also
open 13-16 hrs.

Casa Paco, Puerta Cerrada 11.   Tel: 366 31 66 ££
A small restaurant behind Plaza Mayor, specializing in quality steak. Or try their Fabada Asturiana – a stew of beans,
sausage and bacon.
Open: 13-16 hrs & 20.30-24.00 hrs. Closed Sun and in Aug.

La Taberna del Prado, Marqués de Cubas
                              Tel: 429 60 41 ££
Very cosy family-run restaurant, friendly atmosphere and
superb, original food. Near Sevilla metro.

Hogar Gallego, Plaza Comandante Morenas 3
Very pleasant in summer as you can eat outdoors. Special-
izes in seafood, Galician cuisine.
Open: 13-16 & 19-23.30 hrs. Closed Sunday nights and most
of August.   Tel: 542 48 26 ££

La Biotica, Amor de Dios (nr. Anton Martin metro, Line 1)
Good restaurant, excellent for vegetarians.
Open: lunchtime and evenings.   £

Hard Rock Café, Plaza Colón/Paseo Castellana.
                              Tel: 435 02 00 £

El Luarques, Ventura de la Vega 16   Tel: 429 61 74 £
Always packed with Madrileños, this restaurant offers very
good value and serves some good Asturian home-cooking
specialities.
Open: 13-16.30 & 21-23.30 hrs. Closed Sunday nights,
Mondays and from July 20 to Sep 1.

MADRID

El Buda Feliz, Tudescas 5 Tel: 531 95 24 £
Just for a change from Spanish cuisine, try this Happy Buddha Chinese restaurant. Pleasant surroundings, cheap and cheerful, in a turning off Gran Vía.
Open: 13-16 & 20-24 hrs. Closed Sunday nights.

Las Cuevas de Luis Candelas, Cuchilleros 1
On the south-west buttress wall of Plaza Mayor, serves real Castilian food, particularly roast lamb and sucking pig. Brimming with atmosphere, like its other near neighbours including Casa Botin.
Open: 13-16 & 19.30-00.30 hrs. Tel: 366 54 28 ££

Meson del Corregidor, Plaza Mayor 8-9
Another characteristic Castilian venue that serves roast lamb and sucking pig, Segovia style.
Open: 13-16 & 21-24 hrs. Tel: 366 50 56 ££

Zarauz, Calle Fuentes 13 Tel: 247 72 70 ££
A Basque restaurant north-west of Plaza Mayor, specializing in sea food. When we visited, the restaurant was packed, and it seemed we were the only non-Spaniards in the place. Lunch included oysters, and shangurro – grilled spider crab.
Open: 13-16 & 20.30-24.00 hrs. Closed Mon and in August.

Fast Food outlets

Burger King, Arenal (just off Puerto del Sol); and Gran Via.

McDonalds, Montera; and Gran Vía

VIPS, numerous branches including Gran Vía 34; Princesa 5; Velázquez 84; and O'Donnell 17.
From breakfast till after midnight, they serve a large variety – pizza, pasta, burgers, steak and chips etc. VIPS also sell newspapers, gifts, records and many other items.
Open: 9-3 hrs.

Cafés
Cafés tend to be rather smart, with waiter service. You can order soft drinks, liqueurs, snacks or simple meals. Usually open from early morning until at least midnight. Here are some reputable chains of cafés which offer good value.

California, at Goya 47; and Gran Vía 39
Manila, at Juan Bravo 37; Goya 5; and Gran Vía 41
Nebraska, at Gran Vía 55 and 32; Bravo Murillo 109; and Alcalá 18.
Café de la Villa, Plaza de Colón

Traditional Cafés

'Traditional' means they look quite unchanged from past decades. They are usually crowded, often frequented by writers and artists who pass the hours in endless discussion.

Café de Oriente, Plaza de Oriente 2
A good place to rest your feet after you've done the Royal Palace.
Café Gijón, Paseo de Recoletos 21
Probably the most famous in Madrid. Tables on the main avenue in summer.
The Embassy, corner of Castellana and Ayala
Very elegant tea-room and pastry shop.
Café Lyon, Alcala 57
Old-fashioned decor with a certain charm and elegance.

Finally, something 'different'

L'Hardy, Carrera de San Jerónimo 8 (near Puerta del Sol)
This very traditional stand-up snack bar offers self-service consommé from a gleaming samovar, and help-yourself croquettes etc. Confess how many you've eaten, at cash desk on the way out.

Museo del Jamon – 'Ham Museums' are scattered all over central Madrid, stacked on walls and ceilings with hundreds of cured hams. Excellent for every kind of ham, salami or cheese sandwich, with choice of hot dishes or a set meal.

2.10 Nightlife

Nightlife in Madrid can be as wild or as relaxing as you wish. There is something to suit all tastes. Discos and flamenco clubs stay open till around 5 a.m., and offer a good night's entertainment. Having had a 'second supper' at 3 a.m., only one breakfast is adequate: the Madrid speciality of 'chocolate con churros'. That's a mug of hot thick drinking-chocolate with fresh doughnuts.

Otherwise, for a quiet evening, bars, cafes, and summertime 'terraces' are ideal for watching the world go by until past midnight. The central streets of Madrid are lively with people until one or two a.m. In general, it's the custom to go out in the evening, even if just for a stroll.

There's pleasure in Spanish-style bar-hopping. Certain areas have stylish bars in which you can sample the local wine or a sparkling *cava*, and listen to piano or jazz music. The busiest areas are around Plaza Mayor, Puerta del Sol, Gran Vía, Paseo de la Castellana, Calle de Huertas and Calle de Princesa.

MADRID

Most establishments stay open till the early hours, and are very popular in summer. The Chueca area around Libertad and Figueroa Streets is gay.

In bar-hopping style, it's fun to pick an area and make your own discoveries. The full choice runs into many hundreds of establishments, but here are a few suggestions.

Champagne Bars
Cava de Liria, San Bernardino 2
Champariat, Velardo 12
Champoll, Apodaca 6
Gala, Moratin 24

Jazz Bars
La Grota, Doctor Cortezo 1
Cafe Berlin, Calle Jacometrezo 4
Central, Plaza de Angel 10

Discos
There are discos in Madrid to suit everyone, though some are quite expensive. The price depends on the disco itself, but there are two systems. In some you pay to enter and the price includes a drink. In others there may be little or no entrance fee, but very high prices are charged for drinks.

Xenos, corner of Gran Vía and Plaza de Callao
Popular disco with a good variety of music. Could be minimum of 3000 ptas including drink.
Joy Eslava, Arenal 11
Very lively and popular in a converted theatre; closes 5 a.m.
Oh! Madrid, Ctra de la Coruna – 5 miles out on Highway N-V1
Best in the summer, a disco with open-air pool and barbeque. Another disco called **Four Roses** is a mile further out on the same road.
Pachá, Barceló 11, near Tribunal metro
Opened in 1980 in Teatro Barceló. Open Wed-Sun only.
Archy, Calle Marqués del Riscal 11 (near R. Dario metro)
Very exclusive, and there may be difficulty in getting past the doorman!

Flamenco
Madrid is renowned for its flamenco shows, and you can be sure of a lively, colourful evening. Some clubs serve dinner, with a price-range of 6,000 to 10,000 ptas, usually including a drink. If you are not dining, reckon around 3,000 ptas, to include a good ration of drink, with no pressure to keep ordering more.

Clubs serving dinner open around 9 p.m. Otherwise 11 p.m. is normal. If dining, it's best to reserve.

Arco de Cuchilleros, Cuchilleros 7   Tel: 266 58 79
One of the less expensive flamenco clubs. Intimate, cosy
club located in the centre of Madrid. Meals not available.
Two shows per evening.
Open: 22.30-02.30 hrs. Metro: Sol.

Corral de la Pacheca, Juan Ramon Jimenez 26
Set on the north side of Madrid, this club offers both fla-
menco and folk dancing. Dinner prices are modest.
Open: 21.30-02.00 hrs.   Tel: 458 11 13

Café de Chinitas, Torrija 7   Tel: 248 51 35
One of the most famous clubs in Madrid. Excellent show
and very good food.
Metro: Santo Domingo

Corral de la Morería, Morería 17 (near crossing of Segovia
and Bailén, south of Royal Palace)   Tel: 265 84 46
An excellent and up-market show, the most famous in Madrid. Drinks are rather expensive. Metro: Opera

Zambra, Velázquez 8   Tel: 575 44 00
Every night an intensely serious flamenco performance from
22.30 to 00.30 hrs. Superb! Entrance includes a drink. An
excellent show, popular with tour groups. Metro: Velázquez.

Scala, Melia Castilla Hotel, Capitan Haya 43
Metro: Cuzco   Tel: 567 50 00
A big-time super-show which includes flamenco and Spanish
ballet. Choice of dinner with bubbly, or drink only. Serves
meals until 22.30 hrs, and shows continue till 3.30 a.m.

Theatres

The Royal Theatre, facing the Royal Palace, was inaugurated in 1850 as a purpose-built Opera House. *See map, fig.
37.* The building closed in 1925 through danger of collapse,
and finally re-opened in 1966 for orchestral concerts. More
recently the theatre has returned to its original function, with
highly advanced technology for opera production.

La Vaguada Theatre is part of a new civic complex next to
Madrid-2, the city's largest shopping mall, located in the
northern suburbs. Symphony concerts are planned.

La Zarzuela Theatre at Jovellanos 3 (Metro: Banco de
España) was built in 1846, using a plan identical to that of
La Scala in Milan. The theatre specialises in zarzuela – a
form of Spanish comic opera that was extremely popular in
the 19th century. *See map, fig. 13.*

2.11 At your service in Madrid

Main Post Office & Telephone
The huge building on Plaza de Cibeles is open Mon-Fri 9-13.30 hrs and 17-19 hrs; Sat 9-14 hrs. Stamps can be bought at any tobacconists. Metro: Banco de España.

Emergency telephone numbers
Police 091 or 092
Fire Brigade 080
Ambulance 2522790

Other phone numbers and addresses

Lost Property
Plaza de Legazpi 7. Tel: 588 4346. Metro: Legazpi.

Medical
Hospital Anglo-Americano, Paseo de Juan XX111, Parque Metropolitano, by Pl. Marqués Comillas. Tel: 234 6700. Metro: Moncloa.

Chemists
For night chemist, a rota is displayed in chemist's windows and the local newspapers. Or tel: 098.

Embassies
British: Fernando el Santo 16. Tel: 419 0200. Open 9-13 hrs, but also open till 18.30 hrs from mid-July till end of September.
American: Serrano 75. Tel: 276 3400.
Canadian: Núñez de Balboa 35. Tel: 431 4300.
Australian: Paseo de la Castellana 143. Tel: 279 8501.
New Zealand: The British Embassy can assist.
Irish: Hermanos Becquer 10. Tel: 225 1685

Tourist Information
Municipal Tourist Information Centre, Plaza Mayor 3. Tel: 266 5477. Open 10-14 hrs and 16-20 hrs weekdays; Sat 10-14 hrs; closed Sun. Metro: Sol.
Plaza de España, Torre de Madrid. Tel: 541 2325. Open 9-19 hrs weekdays; Sat 9.30-13.30 hrs; closed Sun. Metro: Plaza de España.
Duque de Medinaceli 2. Tel: 429 4951. Open 9-19 hrs weekdays; Sat 9-13 hrs; closed Sun. Metro: Gran Vía; Sevilla.
Chamartín Station. Tel: 315 9976. Open 8-20 hrs weekdays; Sat 8-13 hrs; closed Sun. Metro: Chamartín.

Chapter Three

Barcelona

3.1 More than sport and business

Barcelona today rates high among the most exciting cities of the Mediterranean seaboard. The setting is ideal: a city with a 2,000-year heritage that merges into the vigorous Catalonian culture of more recent centuries. Artists and musicians such as Picasso, Joan Miró, Albeniz, Casals and Carreras have been closely linked with Barcelona, which takes fierce pride in a cultural rivalry with Madrid.

Since 1989, Barcelona has established a series of Autumn Festivals that cover all styles of music from classical to jazz, theatre, dance and the performing arts in general. The aim is to position Barcelona among European cities that have well-established music and theatre festivals – Salzburg, Vienna, Edinburgh and the rest.

All the city's main venues – refurbished or newly constructed – are used for top international performances with famed artists and companies. Typical is the new National Theatre of Catalonia, purpose built on a former railway site now called Plaça de les Arts.

Opposite, the Auditorium can offer audience capacity of 2600 for symphony concerts, and a smaller hall of 700 capacity for chamber music. The Auditorium is the permanent base for the Barcelona City Orchestra, with a museum of music and a Centre of Advanced Music Studies.

Meanwhile, the Palau de la Música Catalana – one of Modernist Barcelona's most impressive buildings, dating from 1908 – remains high on any music-lover's agenda. *See map, fig. 12.* The architecture, sculpture, paintings and applied arts make this magnificent concert hall an art gallery in itself. During concert intervals, many of the audience skip the line-up for refreshments and use the time to look closer at all the myriad decorative details.

Barcelona's museums are rich in Catalonian culture, which is quite separate from the rest of Spain. The city's splendid collection of Romanesque and Gothic treasures in the Museum of Catalan Art is a reminder of Catalonia's close ties to medieval European culture. *See map, fig. 22.*

BARCELONA

During the 19th century, Barcelona achieved great prosperity as the first Spanish city to launch into the Industrial Revolution. Hence the ambitious city-planned Extension to the original walled town – an Extension which still serves as the basic model even into the 21st century.

During Franco's time, when Catalonia was out of favour, the city became run-down and shabby, and the 19th-century industrial zone along the foreshore became a derelict rustbelt.

In more recent years, however, Barcelona has again begun to sparkle, with inner-city renewal that earns international architectural awards. In 1991 the Urban Design School of Harvard University honoured Barcelona for its series of redevelopment schemes implemented between 1981 and 1987. The award was given for its "positive contribution to improving the quality of urban life."

When Barcelona succeeded in its bid to host the 1992 Olympic Games, an urgent deadline was automatically created. It's normal that every Olympic city takes the opportunity to upgrade its sport facilities, build new hotels, and construct an Olympic Village for later use as residential accommodation. But Barcelona went far, far beyond those basic objectives.

As the supreme sporting event, the Olympics also provided a classic opportunity for re-shaping the city. During recent decades, numerous detailed projects had been prepared for major schemes to modernize the infrastructure. But mostly they had gathered dust in the archives, through lack of funds to implement the more ambitious plans. Thanks to the Olympics deadline, they suddenly became feasible.

In the words of Barcelona's mayor, the Olympics provided the 'excuse' for putting blueprints into reality, aimed to leave a permanent improvement in the quality of life, and thrust Barcelona forward as one of the Mediterranean's leading cities. The ensuing programme of public works, together with substantial private-sector investments, have cost at least five billion pounds.

Even so, that represents only a starting point. It's the first big instalment towards fulfilment of a "Barcelona 2000 Strategic Plan" which aims to consolidate the city's position among the most dynamic centres of the Mediterranean.

Historically, in medieval times Barcelona rivalled Venice and Genoa in wealth and trading power. In the years leading up to the Games, the dream of a regenerated Catalan capital was realised in a great onslaught of construction which turned Barcelona into Europe's biggest building site.

The most inspiring project was the Parc de Mar area of foreshore where the Olympic Village took shape.

During the early 19th century, the Industrial Revolution steamed into Barcelona along a railway that linked the city with France. Following the last few miles of coastline, the tracks took the simplest route into the city, hugging the shore. Smoke-stack industry then clustered along the line of rail, conveniently discharging all effluent onto the foreshore.

After more than a century of disregard for the environment, the entire area had become totally derelict. The railway fenced off the beach, and access was difficult and unsavoury. Effectively Barcelona was forced to turn its back on the sea, and look instead to the semi-circular backdrop of mountains.

Today, all that area has been cleared and the railway line re-routed. In place is the stylish Olympic Village which converted after the Games into an up-market seaside residential area beside a superb Marina. Several miles of blue-flag beaches, man-made with cargoes of sand, are the basis of a new seafront in the style of Nice or Cannes.

A new coastal highway runs along cuttings and through tunnels to avoid the former railway problem of fencing off the shoreline from the residential and service areas. Former wasteland is blossoming into a tree-shaded pedestrian promenade backed by public parks and sport fields.

Two skyscraper towers – 136 metres high, the tallest in Barcelona – overlook the new Marina and yachting harbour. One tower is the five-star 460-room Hotel Arts; the other is devoted to prestigious offices. The Olympic port below is designed for yachting events, and enjoys high rating among Mediterranean marinas.

Forming part of the harbour, a Conference Centre occupies a platform of reclaimed land. The main auditorium seats 1,500 persons. Added to existing convention facilities, the target is that Barcelona should move up the league table to rank as number five among Europe's conference venues.

A so-called Mountain Beltway now completes a ring road around the city, so that through traffic no longer grinds through the centre. The new highway system enables thousands of commuters to enter and leave Barcelona daily without causing traffic jams. Likewise Barcelona is being linked by high-speed trains with the French TGV system, to integrate into the European network at Toulouse.

To summarise: the impetus of the Games ensured that structural works were carried out in four or five years, instead of being spread over ten or fifteen. The momentum will continue into next century. Take all the improvements together, and Barcelona can rank high as a European city of the future.

The Cultural Olympiad also became the motive power behind an ambitious programme of historical landmarking and preservation, to create a greater awareness of the city's artistic and monumental heritage from Roman and Medieval times.

BARCELONA

In preparation for the Games, Barcelona greatly expanded and upgraded its sporting facilities, particularly in the four main city areas where most of the events were held. The principal events, including the opening and closing ceremonies, took place on the plateau of Montjuïc Mountain which overlooks Barcelona like an Acropolis. An 'Olympic Ring' was laid out with sport venues on a three-level terrace.

Faced with the large investments required, the aim was that everything built for the 16-day Games should have an economic use afterwards.

Typically, the superb 17,000-capacity Palau Sant Jordi sports hall was designed for almost any sport – boxing, tennis, indoor athletics, basketball, ice skating. *See map, fig. 24.* A stage is easily erected for theatrical performances and concerts. The hall has been in use almost every week since it was inaugurated in 1990 with a recital by Pavarotti.

The Olympic Stadium itself was originally built to coincide with Barcelona's 1929 International Exhibition. That was the last major spurt of development on Montjuïc. On the lower slopes are Trade Fair grounds and exhibition halls which still flourish. Further up is the National Palace Museum of Catalan Art and a Poble Espanyol – Spanish Village - which have thrived ever since as tourist highlights.

In the Spanish Village, streets and squares feature a lighthearted tour of every regional building style, with craft workers, shops, bars and restaurants that offer all the colour and vivacity of travel-poster Spain. Day or night, it's worth several hours of anyone's time. *See map, fig. 21.*

Add all these varied ingredients together – sport, business, culture, history, cuisine and a vibrant local lifestyle. If you were last in Barcelona several years ago, be prepared for some delightful surprises!

3.2 Arrival & Public Transport

The airport is located 7 miles south-west of the city. For public transport into Barcelona, turn left after leaving Customs, and follow train symbols and signs marked RENFE, to the extreme end of the terminal.

Moving walkways then take you to the station, where trains operate every 30 minutes between 06.30 and 23.00 hrs to Barcelona-Sants Station. The journey, with two intermediate stops, takes 20 minutes and costs 300 ptas on weekdays, or 345 ptas on Sundays and Bank Holidays. Sants Central Station is amply supplied with taxis and buses, and is on the Metro system. Night-time, when trains are not operating, an occasional RENFE bus does the journey.

There's also a half-hourly bus service EA to Avinguda del Paral-lel, just off Plaça de Espanya. Taxis cost over £10 by the time airport and luggage supplements are added.

Metro

On a brief visit to Barcelona, the Metro system is the easiest public transport to use. Six subway lines offer an excellent service to most corners of Barcelona. Stations are marked with the letter 'M' on a white background, inside a red diamond. Lines are numbered L1 to L5, and an 'S' shape on its side for a service from Catalunya to the northern outskirts of the city. Hours are Mon-Fri 05-23 hrs, but until 01 hrs on weekends and holidays. On Sundays some Metro exits and entrances are closed. Don't worry, the system hasn't shut down! Just look around for another entrance.

Buses

More than 50 bus routes cover all Barcelona, with average frequency of about 6 minutes. Generally they run from 6.30 to 22 hrs, but many lines operate somewhat later, or even on a 24-hour basis.

Buses are colour coded:
Red buses pass through or originate in the city centre.
Yellow buses cross the city, but not through the centre.
Green are peripheral lines.
Blue are night services, all crossing or originating in the city centre.
Buses identified with more than two numbers or by letters are inter-town buses.
Ask for the excellent bus and metro map published free by TMB – Transport Barcelona Metropolitana.

Fares

Single tickets, valid any distance on city buses and the Metro system, cost a standard fare of 125 ptas or a little more on Sundays. Best buy is a multi-journey card – the T-1 – costing 660 ptas, giving you ten trips valid on buses, the Metro, the blue tramway at Tibidabo, the Generalitat's urban rail service, and the Monjuïc cable car (funicular). As you pass through the Metro turnstile, the machine bites off a sector of the card until you've had your ten rides. A couple can share a card. A slightly cheaper 10-ride T-2 is available at 640 ptas, but is not valid on buses.

Tourist Transport Bus

This bus does a regular circuit from Pl. Catalunya, Passeig de Gràcia, Sagrada Família, Güell Park, Av. del Tibidabo, Sants Station, Pl. Espanya, Spanish Village, Olympic Stadium, Miró Foundation, Columbus Monument, Port Vell, Olympic Village, the Zoo, Rambla and the Gothic Quarter.

A one-day ticket permits unlimited use of the bus, enabling you to jump on and off wherever you wish. The service operates 9.00-21.30 hrs daily from April 1 until late October. There's a maximum of 20 minutes between buses.

BARCELONA - Key to maps

Central Barcelona

1 – Plaça de Catalunya
2 – Boqueria food market
3 – Palau Güell, Theatre Arts Museum
4 – Plaça Reial
5 – Columbus column
6 – Drassanes Medieval Shipyards
7 – *Santa Maria* replica; Golondrina pleasure boats
8 – Port Vell: Aquarium and IMAX cinema
9 – Santa Eulalia Cathedral
10 – Torre del Rey Martin; City History Museum
11 – Plaça de Sant Jaume; Generalitat and City Hall
12 – Palau de la Música Catalana
13 – Picasso Museum
14 – General Post Office
15 – Stock Exchange
16 – Textile Museum
17 – Modern Art Museum
18 – Natural History Museum
19 – 'Block of Discord' – modernist architecture, including a Gaudí building

Montjuïc Hill

20 – International Fair exhibition halls
21 – Poble Espanyol – 'Spanish Village'
22 – Museum of Catalan Art
23 – Archaeology Museum
24 – Olympic Ring sports complex
25 – Olympic Stadium
26 – Joan Miró Foundation gallery
27 – Montjuïc Castle, and Military Museum
28 – Attractions Park fun fair

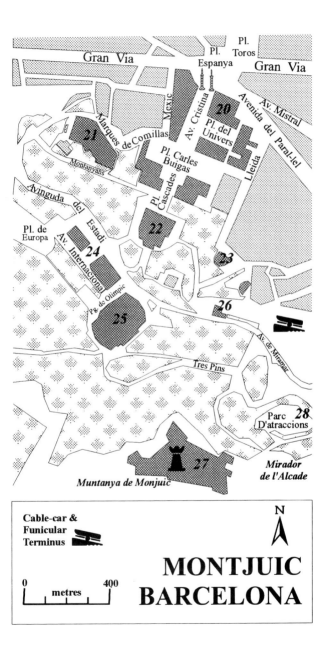

Cable-car &
Funicular
Terminus

N

0 metres 400

MONTJUIC
BARCELONA

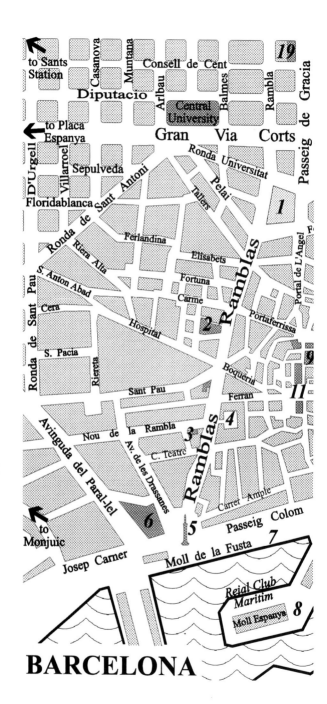

BARCELONA

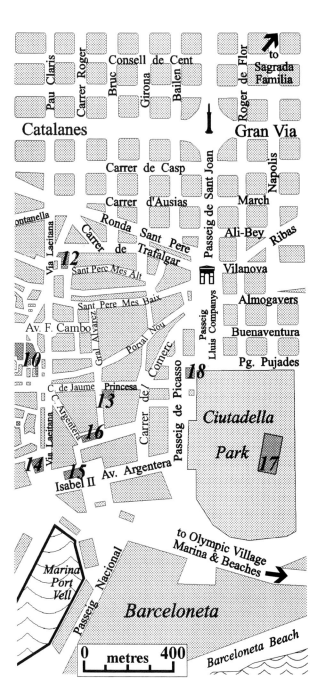

BARCELONA

An excellent free city map is published by the Barcelona Tourist Office. Open it out fully to get the layout.

Starting from the harbour waterfront and going clockwise, pick out the downtown area marked by a squashed hexagon shape of main roads: Paral-lel; Ronda de Sant Pau; Ronda de Sant Antoni; Ronda de la Universitat and Ronda de Sant Pere; Arco del Triunfo and Paseo de Picasso; Passeig d'Isabel 11 and Passeig de Colom.

Fix the shape in your mind. Within that area was the Barcelona of past centuries, bounded by a city wall. That's where you'll find every item of historic interest. Dead centre is the Cathedral *(see map, fig. 9)*, surrounded by the Gothic Quarter, pure Middle Ages but built on Roman foundations.

Carving across the hexagon – from portside Columbus Column and the Drassanes medieval shipyards up to the Plaça de Catalunya – is the famous mile-long promenade called The Ramblas. *See map, between figs. 5 and 1.*

From early 19th century, Barcelona faced a big population explosion due to the Industrial Revolution. Much more space was needed, beyond the tight confines of the original city walls. In 1857 the city planners tore down those outdated defences, and spread out across the plain to the background mountain foothills.

The extension called 'Eixample' or 'Ensanche' was laid out on a ruler-straight city grid system, which remains as Barcelona's basic layout today. A broad avenue called Diagonal slices across from the university and sports area in the northwest of the city, down towards the sea in south-east.

Focal-point of the city is the Plaça de Catalunya *(see map, fig. 1)*. This enormous square is the best starting point for exploring Barcelona. Plaça de Catalunya is easily reached on three subway lines and about a dozen bus services.

Southwards leads into the heart of Old Barcelona. North takes you along the Passeig de Gràcia *(see map, fig. 19)*, which is like a mini Champs Elysees. Some of the wealthiest families of Barcelona built palatial homes along this boulevard, which now is mainly occupied by major companies, banks and luxury shops. Here's the basic starting-point for visitors interested in the turn-of-the-century architecture of Modernism, with Gaudí as the flag-bearer.

In the southwest corner of the map rises Montjuïc Hill, quite innocent of any residential development, but developed as a major area for Olympic sports, family recreation and culture.

Finally along the seafront, going east from Barceloneta is the Olympic Village, Olympic Harbour and Marina, and several miles of Blue Flag beaches. This is where you discover that Barcelona doubles as a Mediterranean resort.

3.4 Basic Barcelona

For the visitor with only a few days to do Barcelona, here's a short list of highlights to capture the flavour of Spain's second city.

(1) Ramble down the Ramblas, and experience the side-street 'tasca' bars.
(2) Explore the Cathedral and its surrounding Gothic Quarter. *See map, figs. 9 & 10.*
(3) View the Sagrada Família building, created by Antoni Gaudí. If you're game for more in the same style, go hunting for the remaining nine buildings in Barcelona built by the same architect.
(4) Spend a whole day on Monjuïc Mountain – seeing the Olympic Ring, choice of five museums, and enjoying the view. Stay on at 'Spanish Village' *(see map, fig. 21)* for evening meal and entertainment.
(5) Have a fish lunch in the Barceloneta district, and take a cross-harbour cable car ride to the Miramar area of Montjuïc for a spectacular overview of the city.
(6) Stroll along the new promenade at Olympic Village and inspect the new Marina and the sandy beaches.
(7) If you like 20th-century art, don't miss the Picasso Museum, Joan Miró Foundation or the Tàpies Foundation.
(8) Visit the Maritime Museum at Drassanes, ride by lift up the Columbus Column, inspect the replica of the *Santa María* if she's in port, and take a Golondrina pleasure-boat ride around the harbour.
(9) Book a half-day excursion to Montserrat.
(10) For music-lovers: get tickets for the Palau de la Música, and enjoy the fabulous decor. *See map, fig. 12.*

Barcelona's Historical Background
City of 2,000,000 population, Barcelona is located on the same latitude as Rome. Founded by the Carthaginians as a trading settlement, Barcelona was developed by the Romans. Traces of that occupation still remain in the city centre. But the biggest reminder of Roman settlement is the Catalan language, based on the Latin dialect spoken by the legions.

In 985 AD Barcelona became capital of Catalonia, which increased dramatically in its power. Around 1100 it became independent, while mountains protected the city from Arab invasion. During the 13th and 14th centuries, Barcelona's influence reached its peak, and the port rivalled Genoa and Venice in its Mediterranean trading wealth.

For a lengthy period Catalonia dominated much of the Mediterranean, spreading over southern France, Balearic Islands and Sardinia. It was among the first nations to have a Parliament, seven years earlier than England. Art and culture flourished.

When Columbus returned from his 1492 voyage of discovery, he reported to Isabella and Ferdinand in Barcelona, dazzling them with talk of gold and silver. But from thence Barcelona's importance slipped, as Mediterranean trade was overtaken by Atlantic trade captured by Cádiz and Seville.

In early 19th century, the Industrial Revolution brought new prosperity to Barcelona. Wealthy patrons helped Barcelona develop as a city of high culture. From mid-19th century, Barcelona lived in an artistic whirl of Catalan Renaissance followed by Modernism and avant-garde art – Gaudí, Picasso, Joan Miró and the rest. The cultural excitement continues.

Sightseeing programme

We suggest dividing up the city, allocating at least half a day to each area:

(1) The Ramblas and the Port
(2) The Gothic Quarter
(3) Montjuïc Hill – up to a full day
(4) Picasso Museum, Cuidadela Park and the new Olympic Harbour and the beaches.
(5) 'The Extension', Modernism and the Gaudí buildings

For each itinerary, the main sights are indicated. But also consider other options listed in section 3.5, to visit if time and inclination permit.

The Ramblas and the Port

La Rambla

Beginning at Plaça de Catalunya *(see map, fig. 1)* and stretching down to the Columbus Monument *(fig. 5)*, this is Barcelona's best known boulevard. All of city life flows along this broad tree-shaded avenue, with flower kiosks and newsstands down the central promenade, and shops, restaurants and bars on both sides and in surrounding side streets.

Here are the main points of sightseeing interest as you stroll down from Catalunya Square:

Palau de la Virreina at No. 99
Boqueria Market off to the right (see shopping section 3.8)
Joan Miró ceramics that pave the Pla de l'Os
Palau Güell, just down Cárrer Nou de la Rambla – a magnificent mansion built by Gaudí, now housing a Museum of Theatre Arts *(see map, fig. 3)*.

The opposite street – Cárrer Colom – leads into the **Plaça Reial**, where Gaudí designed two lamp-posts. The arcaded Royal Square *(see map, fig. 4)* is a delight with its central fountain, palm trees, pigeons and people, and restaurants and café-bars all around. On Sundays there's a morning stamp and coin market. Watch your belongings while you're taking pictures.

Back on the Rambla towards the port, literary standards at the newsstands and bookstores decline, and you enter the red light, transvestite, bag-snatch and pickpocket zone of Barrio Chino. The clientele at many of the side-street bars is somewhat less than genteel.

The **Wax Museum** is close to Drassanes Metro station (see museum section 3.5).

Monument a Colom – Columbus Monument

Claimed to be the tallest monument to Columbus in the world. *See map, fig. 5.* A lift inside will whisk you to the top for a splendid panoramic view of Barcelona.
Operates from 24 June to 24 September, 9-21 hrs; otherwise open 10-14 and 15.30-18.30 hrs Tue to Sat, and 10-19 hrs on Sun and holidays.

Reials Drassanes – Medieval Shipyards

Maritime Museum, Pl. Portal de la Pau, Drassanes
Located in a massive Gothic building from the medieval dock-yards, with seven bays dating pre-Columbus from 14th century and three from 17th century. The museum covers the history of navigation, with ship models and a fine collection of old maps including one used by Amerigo Vespucci.

The prime exhibit is the Galera Real – the royal galley - a beautifully decorated 237-ton replica. The original helped defeat the Turks at Lepanto in 1571. Almost 200 feet long, the red and gold galley was powered by 150 oarsmen. Also try the Sea Adventure, with headphones to enjoy a storm-tossed sailing-ship cruise to Cuba or to explore the seabed.
Open: 10-19 hrs. Closed: Mon. Entrance 600 ptas.
Metro: Drassanes. *See map, fig. 6.*   Tel: 318 3245

Moll de la Fusta

This broad promenade *(see map, fig. 7)* along the inner harbour has been restored by the city. Close to the Columbus Column is the home base of the replica caravel *Santa María*. To mark the 500th anniversary of the Columbus voyage, the vessel sailed in 1991 on a Caribbean itinerary and thence through Panama Canal to Japan – to complete the explorer's dream of finding a sea route to the Orient. More modestly, you can make one-hour Golondrina motor-launch cruises round the harbour.

Port Vell

A new leisure and recreation centre *(see map, fig. 8)* now replaces the former derelict warehouses. Bars, restaurants and shopping centres are trend-setters. Among the attractions

BARCELONA

are a 3-D Imax cinema and a fabulous **Aquarium** on the Moll d'Espanya where visitors can travel on moving walkways through shark-infested waters. The largest aquarium in Europe, it displays 300 species in 20 vast themed tanks. Open 10-21 hrs daily, 10-22 hrs weekends. Entrance 1300 ptas; 950 ptas for under-12s and over-65s. Tel: 221 7474.

La Barceloneta – Little Barcelona
The harbour waterfront continues round to La Barceloneta, with its good seafood restaurants. Across the water there's a panorama of Barcelona town, Monjuïc Hill, and of the cable-car which crosses the harbour. In the background are the surrounding mountains. The cable-car offers an even more dramatic bird's-eye view, swinging you over to Monjuïc.

The Gothic Quarter
Starting from Catalunya Square, go along the shopping street Portal de l'Angel into Plaça Nova, which brings you to the early 13th-century Bishop's Palace on the right, and Cathedral left. *See map, fig. 9.*

Santa Eulalia Cathedral
Dedicated to the city's patron saint, the gothic-style cathedral is 600 years old. Its delicate spires and stained glass windows are stunning. Most memorable are the cathedral cloisters, where squawking geese patrol the inner garden. A Chapter House museum is open 11-13 hrs, entrance 50 ptas.

In the narrow balconied streets around the cathedral, you can leave the 20th century behind and – apart from a few parked cars and motor-bikes – imagine yourself into the Middle Ages. By the northeast corner of the cathedral is the Frederic Marès Museum (see museum section 3.5).

Much further back in time are remains at Cárrer Paradis 10, which are part of the Roman Temple of Augustus. Still richer history is located in Plaça del Rei, where Columbus was received in the 14th-century Royal Palace on returning from his first voyage to the New World. The **Torre del Rey Martin - King Martin's Lookout Tower** – rises five storeys above the hall, and provides a good vantage point. On one side of the square is the City History Museum (see museum section 3.5). *See map, fig. 10.*

Civic administration is centred on the Plaça de Sant Jaume - originally the Roman agora – with palatial buildings on a cobbled square where local citizens dance the Sardana on Sunday evenings. *See map, fig. 11.*

Palau de la Generalitat is home of Catalonia's autonomous government, and dates from 15th century. Open: Sun 10-14 hrs. **Casa de la Ciutat** - City Hall, facing the Palau de la Generalitat, is even older and is a brilliant example of medieval Barcelonian architecture.

Montjuïc Mountain and the Olympic Ring

The area is best approached from Plaça d'Espanya. (Metro: Espanya). Emerging from the subway onto a very large square, head towards twin red-brick towers that look like Italian bell-towers. The broad avenue ahead – Reina María Cristina – is lined with buildings of Barcelona Trade Fair, dating from 1929. *See map, fig. 20.*

From here it's all uphill, the last weary Marathon stretch to the Olympic Stadium. Better strategy is to take a bus to wherever you want to start your visit, and then gradually walk down.

Bus 61 serves Spanish Village (Poble Espanyol); the Olympic Ring and Palau Nacional; Joan Miró Foundation; the funicular station from Paral-lel on Metro line 3; the cable-car to the Castle and its Military Museum; and the Montjuïc amusement park.

If you're just going to Spanish Village, a free London-style double-decker shuttles between Plaça d'Espanya and Poble Espanyol every half hour. If you don't want to wait, catch bus 13 or 61.

Otherwise, walking uphill in a straight line brings you to the Plaça de Carles Buigas where illuminated fountains perform Thu, Sat & Sun from 21 hrs till midnight in summer season; or 20-23 hrs Sat & Sun in winter except January-March.

Poble Espanyol – Spanish Village

Built 1929 for the International Exhibition, to display the buildings, squares and streets typical of different areas of Spain, the Poble Espanyol is still a major attraction to Spaniards and visitors alike. *See map, fig. 21.*

You need several hours to explore it thoroughly, with photo opportunities everywhere you look, craft workshops and shops, restaurants and bars galore.

Typical is the Barrio Andaluz, which creates the atmosphere of Andalusia, somewhat like the Santa Cruz area of Seville. All the houses are whitewashed, with pots of hanging flowers, balconies and the sound of typical music. Bars serve Andalusian food and drink, and there are flamenco shows at night. Don't miss the audio-visual show called Barcelona Experience, giving an overview of the city's history, customs and excitement.

The Olympic Ring

Here was the main setting for the 1992 Olympics – a complex of sports facilities that includes the 70,000-capacity Olympic Stadium, the general-purpose Palau Sant Jordi sports hall designed by a Japanese architect, and ancillary venues for swimming, wrestling, show jumping and other sports. *See map, fig. 24.*

BARCELONA

In the park areas of Montjuïc Hill – below the Olympic Ring – are more sport facilities, a 2000-capacity Greek Theatre, and several museums including the major Museum of Catalan Art, Archeological Museum, and the Ethnological Museum. (see details in section 3.5).

Museum of Catalan Art, Montjuïc Palace   Tel: 423 7199
Contains an important Romanesque art collection from 11th to 13th centuries; Catalan-Gothic art; and Spanish and European baroque. The National Palace has been refurbished by the Italian architect who master-minded the Musée d'Orsay in Paris.
Open: Tue-Sun 10-19 hrs. Entrance 300 ptas. Metro: Espanya. *See map, fig. 22.*

Miró Foundation, Plaça Neptuno, Montjuïc Tel: 329 1908
A dazzling white building, designed by the distinguished international architect Josep Serp. *See map, fig. 26.* The Centre of Contemporary Art Studies was founded by the abstract and surrealist painter Joan Miró, with art exhibition rooms, a library and archives, and also terraces for outdoor exhibits. Occasional chamber music concerts are given.

Opened when the artist was 82 years old, the Foundation contains many of Miró's paintings, way-out tapestries and ceramics. Every room is bursting with highly imaginative ideas, often with a splash of humour.

In more sombre mood is the so-called 'Barcelona Series' – begun in 1939 and published in 1944 – a stark black-and-white series of fifty lithographs which can be considered as Miró's artistic commentary on the Spanish Civil War.

After the artist's death on Christmas Day 1983, the Foundation decided to include works by artists who were friends of Miró or who admired his work. There's a splendid bronze reclining figure from 1953 by Henry Moore, conceived as a personal homage to Miró.
Open: Tue-Sat 11-19 hrs; on Thursday until 21.30 hrs; Sun & hols 10.30-14.30 hrs. Entrance: 600 ptas. Metro: Espanya and Bus 61.

Picasso, Cuidadela Park and Olympic Village
Picasso Museum, Montcada 15-19   Tel: 319 6310
Housed in the medieval palace of Berenguer de Aguilar, this is one of the world's most important museums devoted to Picasso's work. *See map, fig. 13.* Don't miss it!

The Museum is especially rich in the earliest Picassos, including over 2000 sketches when he was still in the classical mode as taught at Barcelona Academy of Fine Arts. By age 15 he had mastered techniques which take most students many years to acquire: light effects, transparency of clothes, perspective. Later periods are well represented, especially

Blue Period and early Cubist, and then a 40-year jump to his 1957 Las Meninas – 58 variations on a Velasquez theme.

In the ceramic section is a joyous collection of ceramics, dating from 1947 onwards. Every plate and pot smiles at you.

Open: Tue-Sat 10-20 hrs; Sun 10-15 hrs. Entrance 500 ptas. Metro: Jaume 1.

Also in Montcada Street are several other mansions, converted to art and cultural centres, including a Costume Museum and the Galeria Maeght.

Cuidadela Park

From the Picasso Museum, along Cárrer de la Princesa leads to Cuidadela Park which provides a refreshing interlude from the city hustle. See the enormous fountain, numerous monuments and statues, a lake and a zoo.

The park also includes the **Museum of Modern Art** *(see map, fig. 17)*, which shares a building with the Catalonian Parliament.

From the park, a seawards direction reaches the Olympic Marina and the four kilometres of superb new beach promenade.

The Gaudí and Modernism circuit

According to tourism surveys, 24 per cent of visitors rate buildings designed by Antoni Gaudí as Barcelona's leading sightseeing attraction. The city has the highest number of Modernist buildings in Europe – 500 of them – even more than Vienna.

Modernism is a variant of the turn-of-the-century movement also known as Art Nouveau, Art Deko or Jugendstil. Barcelona's most individualistic flag-bearer of this style was Antoni Gaudí. He was born 1852 and based his working life on Barcelona, where he was killed by a tram in 1926. His most controversial building, still under construction, is the **Sagrada Família** cathedral which features on all city sightseeing tours.

Work started in 1882. Construction has been very slow, partly due to a policy of funding the project only though anonymous donations. The towers and two secondary facades are now built – a complete sculpture gallery, like a book in stone portraying the life of Christ.

Work still continues on the main 'Glory Facade' devoted to the Passion. The selected sculptor works with "negative volumes", often more Gaudínian than Antoni Gaudí himself. An on-site museum displays plans, models and history of the building.

Open: 9-19 hrs or later in summer. Entrance: 700 ptas. Metro: Sagrada Família.

BARCELONA

The 'Block of Discord', Passeig de Gràcia

On this city block are three delightful examples of Modernist architecture. Go early morning, like 8.30 in summer, or 9.30 in winter to photograph the facades in sunshine. (Metro: Passeig de Gràcia brings you to the doorstep). *See map, fig. 19.*

Casa Battlo at no. 43 is a typical Gaudí renovation of the facade and the inner staircase. Ceramics and multi-coloured glass mosaics depict the legend of St. George (patron saint of Catalonia) and the Dragon. Skull-like iron balconies and bone columns represent victims of the dragon.

Go inside to see the staircase, with a balustrade that resembles the lower part of a dragon's spinal column. Wall tiles gradually change from light blue at the bottom to dark blue nearer the sky. Everything is wavy, not a straight line anywhere.

Look at no. 41 next door. The Casa Amattler was built by Puig i Cadafalch, another respected architect in Modernist style. Mixture of Flemish with medieval Gothic, the building is decorated with ceramic tiles and innumerable motifs based on Nature. Again, look inside at the splendid carriage entrance and staircase.

At no. 35 is the Tourist Board HQ, the Casa Lleo-Morero by Montaner, who also built the landmark building around the corner at Aragó 255 (now used by the Antoni Tàpies Foundation – see section 3.5).

Casa Milà – La Pedrera

At no. 92 Passeig de Gràcia is the fantastic apartment building nicknamed La Pedrera – the Quarry. Gaudí's design is based on organic themes from Nature. Especially remarkable are the balconies and the roof, with total absence of straight lines.

The roof is accessible – free but no lift – from Mon-Fri, on the hour at 10, 11, 12 and 13; and at 16, 17 and 18 hrs. Sat amd Sun are morning only. You can easily use a roll of film, taking pictures of the most incredible chimney-pots.

Parque Güell

Best way to the park is by taxi. Otherwise, take subway to Lesseps on the green line; then walk or take taxi.

This unusual and inventive park was originally conceived as a real estate project by Count Güell and Gaudí, but was bought by the city in 1929. The Disney-type fantasy is typical of Gaudí's creative talent, witty and original.

The upper market place is used for performances of Sardana - usually on Sundays. Look at the winding line of benches, decorated with recycled tiles and designed so that people can talk to each other in privacy.

In the park is the **House-Museum**, where Gaudí lived

from 1906 to 1926. On show are his personal effects, drawings and plans; and his own architect-designed furniture. The house was declared a historic and artistic monument of national interest in 1969.

Open: Sun-Fri 10-14 & 16-18 hrs, and until 19 hrs Apr-Sep. Entrance 200 ptas. Metro: Lesseps.

Palau de la Música Catalana

Location of the concert hall is Amadeu Vives 1, just off the Via Laietana.

The most magnificent Modernist concert hall in Europe, built by Domenech Montaner. Any music-lover who cannot attend a concert should at least see the fabulous Art Deco interior on tours which have recently been organised on Tue, Wed and Fri.

To check on timing, call 268 4010 or 268 1000. Otherwise just walk in to the foyer, visit the bar, look at the collection of Catalan and Majorcan bagpipes, and admire the staircase. It's truly a Palace of Mosaic, built and decorated by the finest Catalan craftsmen.

Metro: Jaume 1. *See map, fig. 12.*

3.5 Other Museums and Galleries

Note: Entrance times and prices may change. On public holidays, some institutions are closed, while others follow Sunday hours. Prices are usually reduced for students and over-65s.

Frederic Marès Museum, Plaça de Sant Iu Tel: 310 5800
Located just by the Cathedral. *See map, fig. 9.* The sculptor's private collection of sculpture from pre-Roman times to the 20th century; also an ethnic collection reflecting everyday life from 15th century onwards.
Open: Tue-Sat 10-17 hrs; Sun 10-14 hrs.
Entrance 300 ptas. Metro: Jaume 1.

Monastery of Pedralbes Museum, Baixada del Monastir 9, at the end of Paseo de Reina Elisenda   Tel: 203 9282
The monastery building itself with its gothic cloister is worth visiting, but it also houses paintings and sculptures which illustrate different ages in the monastery history. Now also houses part of the Thyssen-Bornemisza collection.
Open: Tue-Sun 10-14.00 hrs; Sat 10-17 hrs. Entrance 300 ptas. Buses: 22, 64, 75. Railway: Reina Elisenda.

Museum of the Theatre Arts, Nou de la Rambla 3
The Palau Güell – another fascinating building designed by Gaudí – houses exhibitions relating to show business. The

BARCELONA

building alone rates a visit. *See map, fig. 3.*
Open: Mon-Sat 11-14 & 17-20 hrs. Metro: Liceu or Drassanes. Tel: 317 5198

Museum of Contemporary Art, Pl. dels Àngels.
MACBA, adjoining the Barcelona Centre of Contemporary
Culture, features a newly established permanent collection
with a year-round programme of temporary exhibitions.
Metro: Catalunya; Universitat. Tel: 412 0810.

Museum of the Arts, Industry and Popular Traditions
(Spanish Village in Monjuïc Park) Tel: 423 0196
Ethnic material, including a reproduction farmhouse from the
Pyrenees and an 18th-century pharmacy.

Museum of Modern Art, La Ciutadella Park
The museum shares the Ciutadella Palace (Palau) with the
Parliament of Catalonia *(see map, fig. 17)*, and features
paintings and sculptures mainly by Catalan artists from late
18th century till today.
Open: Tue-Sun 10-19 hrs. Entrance 300 ptas.
Metro: Arc de Triomf; Barceloneta. Tel: 319 5728

Museum of Pictorial Art, Poble Espanyol (Spanish Village
in Monjuïc Park) Tel: 426 1999
Displays the techniques of pictorial art.
Open: Mon-Fri 9-14 hrs.

Music Museum, Avinguda Diagonal 373 Tel: 416 1157
Housed in a Modernist building which itself is worth seeing.
String and wind instruments from around the world, 16th to
20th century, and including exotic instruments from the East
and Latin America. The collection of guitars is of world
class, but explanations are only in Castilian and Catalan.
Open: Tue-Sun 10-14 hrs; Wed 17-20 hrs. Entrance 300
ptas. Metro: Diagonal.

Palace of Pedralbes Museum, Avinguda Diagonal 686
Formerly the residence of King Alfonso X111, the palace
houses a valuable tapestry and rug collection, decorative arts
and crafts, and a Carriage Museum. In the same location is
a Ceramics Museum including pieces by Miró and Picasso.
Open: Tue-Sun 10-14 hrs. Entrance 300 ptas.
Metro: Palau Reial. Tel: 208 5024

Tàpies Foundation, Aragó 255 Tel: 487 0315
Formerly a publishing house, one of Barcelona's first Modernist style buildings, the premises are now devoted to exhibitions of contemporary art. The foundation was created by
the Catalan painter Antoni Tàpies in 1984, as a scholarly

centre and library for the understanding of modern art and culture. For modern art lovers, it is something special. On the roof is a controversial wirescape sculpture called "Chair on Clouds", which looks better by night, when lit up.
Open: Tue-Sun 11-20 hrs. Entrance 400 ptas. Metro: Passeig de Gràcia.

Thyssen Bornemisza Foundation, 9 Baixada Monestir.
An exhibition of 72 paintings and 8 sculptures from this great private collection, covering Italian and north-European art from 13th to 18th centuries, housed in the Pedralbes Monastery.   Tel: 280 1434
Open: 10-14 hrs; Sat 10-17 hrs; closed Mon. Entrance 300 ptas. Railway: Reina Elisenda. Bus 22, 64, 75, 114.

Museum of the History of the City – Casa Clariana Padellas, Plaça del Rei *(see map, fig. 10).*   Tel: 315 1111
In the basement are relics from Barcelona's Roman times. The Gothic-style building itself dates from the 15th century. Work up through three floors of local history, illustrated with paintings, ceramics, documents and prints.
Open: Tue-Sat 9-14 & 16-20 hrs; Sun 9-13.30 hrs. Entrance 300 ptas. Metro: Jaume 1.

Archaeological Museum, Passeig Sta. Madrona, Montjuïc Park   Tel: 423 2149
Located in the former Palace of Graphic Arts, built for the 1929 International Exhibition. *See map, fig. 23.* Covers Prehistoric times to the 7th century AD, in the Iberian Peninsula and Balearics. The Roman mosaics are outstanding.
Open: Tue-Sat 9.30-13.30 hrs & 15.30-19.00 hrs; Sun 10-14 hrs. Entrance 200 ptas, Sun free.
Metro: Espanya plus bus 55, 61.

Ethnological Museum, Avinguda Santa Madrona, Montjuïc Park   Tel: 424 6402
Ranges worldwide, including objects from pre-Columbus Americas.
Open: 10-14 hrs. Tue & Thu 10-17 hrs; closed Mon. Entrance 300 ptas. Metro: Espanya plus bus 13 or 55.

Military Museum, Montjuïc Castle   Tel: 329 8613
Military hardware and documents, model castles and military uniforms. *See map, fig. 27.*
Open: Tue-Sun 9.30-13.30 & 15.30-19.30 hrs. Entrance 200 ptas. Metro: Espanya plus bus 61.

Botanical Gardens, Parc del Migdia
Devoted to cultivation of the main species of the five regions of the world which have a Mediterranean climate.

BARCELONA

Footwear Museum, Museu del Calçat, Plaça de Sant Felip Neri   Tel: 301 4533
In the former HQ of the Shoemakers Guild, a collection of shoes across the centuries.
Open: Tue-Sun 11-14 hrs. Entrance 200 ptas. Metro: Jaume 1.

Holographic Museum, Plaça de Sant Jaume Tel: 310 2172
Demonstrates holographic techniques and applications. *See map, fig. 11.*
Open: Mon-Sat 10.30-13.30 & 17.30-20.30 hrs. Entrance 100 ptas. Metro: Jaume I.

Museum of Funeral Carriages, Almogávares
A change from the usual transport museum. Tel: 484 1720
Open: Mon-Fri 9-14 hrs. Entrance free. Metro: Marina.

Perfume Museum, Passeig de Gràcia 39   Tel: 216 0146
Scent bottles and cosmetics containers from antiquity to the present day.
Open: Mon-Fri 10-13.30 & 16-19 hrs. Entrance free.
Metro: Passeig de Gràcia.

Mechanical Doll Museum – Museu d'Automats del Tibidabo, Mount Tibidabo Amusement Park   Tel: 211 7942
Something different: a collection of mechanical dolls in human and animal form, housed in a turn-of-the-century Modernist building.
Open: in summer 11-20 hrs; winter Sat & Sun only, 11-20 hrs. Train to Av. Tibidabo, then tram and funicular to a splendid mountain view 1650 feet above Barcelona. The amusement park makes a popular Sunday excursion for the locals.

Textile and Garment Museum, Montcada 12-14
In the gothic palace of the Marquès de Llió, collections of textiles from the 4th century onwards, garments from the past 300 years, and contemporary creations.
Open: Tue-Sat 10-17; Sun 10-14 hrs. Entrance 300 ptas.
Metro: Jaume 1.   Tel: 310 4516

Wax Museum – Museu de Cera, Pasaje de la Banca 7, Rambla de Sta. Monica   Tel: 317 2649
A Barcelona-type Madame Tussauds with over 360 famous people in appropriate settings with projecstions and sound effects. Housed in a building of artistic and historic interest, near the bottom end of the Ramblas.
Open: Mon-Fri 10-13.30 & 16.00-19.30; Sat-Sun until 20 hrs; summer 10-20 hrs. Entrance 750 ptas.
Metro: Drassanes.

Barcelona Football Club Museum, Stadium at Avinguda
Aristides Maillol   Tel: 330 9411
The world-famed club's history and trophies, with a 5-screen
video show. View the stadium from the Presidential box.
Open: Apr-Oct Mon-Sat 10-13 and 15-18 hrs; Nov-Mar Tue-
Fri 10-13 & 15-18 hrs; Sat & Sun 10-14 hrs. Entrance 400
ptas. Metro: Collblanc.

Bullfighting Museum – Museu Taurí, Monumental Bullring,
Gran Via Corts Catalanes 749   Tel: 245 5803
Two rooms with trophies, branding-irons, posters, costumes
of famous bullfighters and heads of celebrated bulls.
Open 10.30-14.00 hrs & 16-19 hrs, during the bullfight
season only. On bullfight days open only 10.30-13 hrs.
Entrance 300 ptas. Metro: Glòries.

Sport Museum – Museu i Centre d'Estudis de l'Esport "Dr.
Colet", Buenos Aires 56-58   Tel: 419 2232
Located near Plaça Francesc Macia and Diagonal, in an Art
Deco building designed by architect Puig I Cadafalch, an
exhibition centre on sporting and Olympic themes.
Open: Mon-Fri 10-14 & 16-19 hrs. Entrance free.

3.6 Take a trip

Barcelona offers several good choices of half-day or whole-
day excursions. North or south are the beach resorts of
Costa Brava or Costa Dorada. Frequent train or bus services
serve all the coastal destinations.

For a ready-planned package, a typical coach excursion
features a drive along dramatic coastal scenery through Bada-
lona, Mataro, Caldetas, Arenya de Mar, Calella de Mar,
Lloret de Mar and Tossa de Mar – the pearl of the Costa
Brava. During summer, weather permitting, a boat cruise
could be included – say, from Tossa and Lloret de Mar to
Fanals with free time for bathing and lunch.

Lloret de Mar, top package resort on the Costa Brava,
features an attractive beach with a palm-lined promenade. It
is very crowded in high summer.

Equally lively is Calella de Mar (closer to Barcelona, on
the Costa Dorada) with pubs, bierkellers and discos galore.
The steeply-shelving beach runs the full length of the town
and miles to the north, while on the southern side there are
rocky headlands and sandy coves.

Modern art fans could make a whole-day trip to Figueres
– the unlikely setting for one of the world's most bizarre
museums, dedicated entirely to the works of Salvador Dalí.

In a different direction – 38 miles north-east from Barcelona – is Montserrat, the great monastery founded in 880, a

legendary home of the Holy Grail. There one can see the fabled 'Black Madonna' – La Moreneta – and listen to the impressive boys' choir and sample monastic liqueurs.

The world-famous shrine is perched high on the Montserrat (Sawtooth) Mountain, 3,725 feet above the Llobregat river valley. This is a mountain of weird shapes formed by erosion and giant masses of rock which assume various colours according to the light. There are splendid views from the monastery, and on a mountain walk from the Hermitage of San Jerónimo.

Most of Costa Dorada is southwest of Barcelona. The long golden-sand beaches have much less scenic interest compared with the 'wild coast'. The most popular resorts are Sitges (famed for its flowers) and Salou (spread out in low-profile style among the pine-woods). The theme park of Port Aventura can be reached in one hour by tour coach from Sants station at 8.30 hrs daily, returning by 21 hrs, and costing about £24 including entrance.

Otherwise, the principal excursion is to Tarragona, which has a very well-preserved Roman city, overlaid by medieval monuments. The Cathedral is built on the site of a Roman temple to Jupiter. Among the former distinguished Roman residents were Emperor Augustus and Pontius Pilate.

3.7 Sunday in Barcelona

Church Services

Most churches are Catholic. Sunday masses are said between 7-14 hrs; evenings between 19-21 hrs. Anglican mass in English – St. George's Church, Sant Joan de la Salle 41. Sun at 11 hrs and Wed at 11.30 hrs. Tel: 417 8867.

Museums & Galleries

Most museums are open Sunday mornings, often until 14 hrs. Check details in sections 4 and 5 of this chapter, before making a special journey.

Shops & Street Markets

These specialized street markets are held every Sunday:
Books and Coins – Ronda de Sant Antoni (Metro Universitat) - 10-14 hrs.
Art – Mostra d'Art, Plaça de Sant Josep Oriol (Metro Liceu) - 11-14.30 hrs. Also operates Saturday 11-20 hrs.
Coins and Postage Stamps – Plaça Reial (Metro Liceu) – 10-14 hrs.

Go folk-dancing

At Plaça de Sant Jaume in the heart of the Gothic district (Metro Liceu or Jaume 1), everyone is invited on Sundays and holidays to join in dancing La Sardana. Check the timings – sometimes the dance is held around noon, otherwise in early evening. In this traditional Catalonian circle dance, people join hands while pacing and retracing the steps in stately fashion. Music is supplied by the 'cobla' – a group of wind instruments accompanied by a double-bass.

Montjuïc & Tibidabo
Choose Sunday for one or other of these hilltop locations, which are then very animated with local families. Especially at Montjuïc there's plenty to keep you occupied all day.

Other Sunday events
In the football season, why not see one of the famous local teams – Español or Barcelona (Barça). Barça's stadium – Camp Nou – can hold 120,000 spectators. The Sarria stadium of Rcal Club Deportivo Español has room for 42,000. Admission prices are between 1,000 and 4,500 ptas.

Bull fights are held Sundays at 17.30 hrs during the season March to September. The venue is the Monumental Bull Ring at Gran Via C.C. 743. (Metro: Glòrias). Local coach tour operators offer a package of shade or sun ticket, transport and a guide to explain the ritual. Otherwise there's a box office at Muntaner 24. (Metro: Universidad).

Take a trip
As some key museums are closed on Mondays, schedule a Sunday-morning city sightseeing tour and save Monday for shopping. The afternoon could then be used for an excursion to Montserrat. Ask the local agent for details.

3.8 Shopping in Barcelona

Shops are open 9-14 and 16-20 hrs or even later. The big department stores stay open from 10 to 20 hrs, or till 21 hrs on Saturdays, with no afternoon closing. Most of the shopping arcades are open 10.30 till 20.30, though around half of them close for the afternoon break.

Mainly there are three shopping zones:

- Diagonal – especially around Plaza de Francesc Macia
- Passeig de Gràcia
- Plaça Catalunya and La Rambla (for souvenirs).

The rival department stores – El Corte Inglés and Galerías Preciados – each have two branches: in Plaça Catalunya and close by in Av. Portal de l'Angel; and at Diagonal 617 and Diagonal 471. Top-floor restaurants and cafeterias are reasonably priced. Go mid-morning for a low-cost cooked breakfast deal which could qualify as an early lunch.

If you want something typically Catalonian, then look out for ceramics. The region also has a productive cottage industry producing rugs and woven goods, glassware, jewelry and other items. Traditional Spanish gifts are easily found in the numerous souvenir stores, and antiques are available at market or from street traders.

At **Artesania** – Passeig de Gràcia 55 – three permanent craft exhibition halls display products of creative Catalonian craftsmen.

Markets

There are plenty of them in Barcelona, especially on Sunday mornings. They are ideal to experience the true Catalan atmosphere, and even to find a bargain. Among the best are:

Mercat de Sant Josep – La Boqueria *(see map, fig. 2)*
Halfway down La Rambla, this 19th-century colonnaded market specialises in mouthwatering Mediterranean displays of fresh fruit and vegetables, meat and seafoods.

Plaça Reial – Royal Square
On Sunday morning this near perfect quadrangle is transformed into a sea of stamp and coin collectors. Definitely worth a visit. *See map, fig. 4.*

Plaça Nova – New Square
An outdoor Sunday market, dating back to the 13th century.

Els Encants
This second-hand flea market, located in Pl. de las Glòrias, is open Mon, Wed, Sat from 8-19 in winter, or 8-20 hrs in summer. (Metro: Glòrias).

Gothic Quarter Antiques Market
Located in Pl. del Pi, is open every Thursday 9-20 hrs except in August.

3.9 Eating Out

Barcelona offers an enormous range of restaurants of all types and prices, with the full range available in the Old Barcelona area. Fish restaurants cluster in the harbour area of La Barceloneta. Other restaurants are bunched in Gràcia (north of Plaça de Catalunya) and along the stretch of Diagonal where many hotels are located.

As a major port and commercial city, Barcelona also offers a wide choice of foreign restaurants of several dozen nationalities.

The local wines of Catalonia range from the bubbly cava wines, produced by the champagne method but far cheaper, to a wide selection of still wines. The sparkling cava wines come in brut and seco dry varieties, with semisecos and dulces (medium and sweet) for dessert.

The pale white Alella wines go well with fish or cheese. Most of the Ampurdan wines are rosé, and are suitable with fish or light meat or pasta dishes. The Catalonian reds are full-bodied. The Penedes region is famed for fine wines, with Miguel Torres as the leading winery.

Catalan specialities

For Catalan cuisine, here's a selection of menu items that you're likely to find in typical Catalan inns – tabernas catalanas. There's an excellent range of local fish and seafood, often served in stews or in paella style. Garlic, tomatoes and peppers are used with abandon.

Espinacas a la catalana – a spinach appetizer with garlic, pine nuts and raisins

Pan tomate – bread with a topping of tomato purée and olive oil, eaten along with many seafood dishes

Bocadillo – bread with varied toppings

Escudella i carn d'olla – a thick vegetable, pork and chicken soup with rice, noodles and potatoes

El cocido – a stew with haricot beans

Botifarra – Catalan sausage

Botifarra amb mongetes – Catalan sausage with beans

Huevos a la catalana – eggs baked on a foundation of minced pork, ham and tomatoes

Tortilla a la barcelonesa – ham and chicken liver omelette, with tomatoes and a spinach sauce

Arros a la cassola – local name for Valencian-type paella

La zarzuela – a musical comedy of a fish and seafood casserole that includes monk fish, prawns, squid and mussels with a splash of wine and rough brandy

Opera – a zarzuela with lobster instead of prawns

Suquet de Peix - another mixed-up fish dish

Bullabesa – local spelling for the Catalan version of bouillabaisse

Bacalla a la llauna – cod cooked in a boiling-pan

Faves a la catalana – lima beans flavoured with herbs

Tapas Bars

For quick snacks try the 'tascas' – bars that specialize in portions of 'tapas' of every description. It's a very sociable institution aimed at fighting off hunger until the restaurants are seriously in business.

On a dedicated tasca-crawl, you can easily pack away enough vitamins for a full meal. Many are found in the streets on either side of La Rambla; around the Plaça Reial; and around the Picasso Museum along Cárrer Princesa and Cárrer Montcada.

In the Barceloneta port area, the **Ramonet** and **Panol** taverns in Cárrer Maquinista are very good. Other popular tapas bars worth trying are:

Alt Heidelberg, Ronda Universitat 5 (Metro: Universitat or Catalunya)
Cerveceria, top of La Rambla, opposite Hostal Continental
La Gran Bodega, Cárrer Valencia, between Muntaner and d'Aribau (Metro: Hospital Clinic)

Cafés
Café Zurich, corner of Pelai and Plaça Catalunya
Oriente, Rambla 45
Café de l'Opéra, Rambla 74 – in 19th-century style
Salon de Te Llibre i Serra, Ronda de Sant Pere (San Pedro) 3 (Metro: Urquinaona)

Fast Food Chains
Burger King, top of La Rambla
McDonald's, Pelai 62 and on corner of Rambla and Ferran
Chicago Pizza Pie Factory, Provença 300 Drugstore David, Tuset 19 (off La Diagonal). Hamburgers, pizzas etc.
El Drugstore, Passeig de Gràcia 71. Open 24 hours a day.
Compagnia General de Sandwiches, Santalo 153 (Metro: Muntaner) and Moya 14 (a little street where Tuset meets Diagonal). Superb selection.

Restaurant Guide
Most restaurants offer adequate choice on their set menu deal, which can be a good moneysaver compared with ordering a la carte. In the Old Barcelona district are dozens of lower-cost establishments with fixed-price menus prominently displayed at the door, or with details chalked on blackboards.

Note that price often reflects the restaurant's facilities more than quality of food. Some of the cheaper restaurants with less elaborate service and decor can provide meals as good and tasty as the more expensive establishments.

The following is a short list of restaurants that you may like to try. You can spend more or less money according to menu choice, but the restaurants have been roughly price-graded to allow for an average complete meal, from gourmet rating to budget.

£££ – £20+
££ – £10-£20
£ – under £10

In Old Barcelona area

Quo Vadis, Calle del Carmen 7   Tel: 302 4072 £££
A highly original restaurant, definitely worth a visit. Try
their sea bass with fennel. Closed Sun and August.
Metro: Liceu

Los Caracoles, Escudellers 14   Tel: 302 3185 ££
Catalan food in the heart of old Barcelona. Don't miss it!
Metro: Liceu or Drassanes.

Can Culleretes, Quintana 15   Tel: 317 6485 ££
Founded in 1786, it follows the traditions of real Catalan
cooking. Located just off the Rambla, between Cárrer
Boqueria and Ferran. Closed Sun evening, Mon and two
weeks in June or July.
Metro: Liceu

Els Quatre Gats, Montsió 3   Tel: 302 4140 ££
Special for Picasso fans – the haunt of the artist and his
friends. In a Modernist building, the restaurant serves Catalonian cuisine. A café section serves snacks.
Metro: Catalunya

Egipte, Jerusalem 3   Tel: 317 7480 £
Excellent value for money, hidden behind the La Boqueria
market. Serves Catalan dishes.
Metro: Liceu

Agut, Gignas 16   Tel: 315 1709 £
Good value Catalan cooking in the Barrio Chino district.
Closed Sun evenings, Mon and July.
Metro: Jaume 1 – walk down Via Laitena, and Cárrer Gig-
nas is close to the big post office.

Self Naturista, Santa Anna 15-17   Tel: 302 2130 £
Very cheap and popular self service vegetarian wholefood
restaurant. Closed Sun and holidays.
Metro: Catalunya – just south of the Plaza.

Around the Harbour district – Metro: Barceloneta

Siete Puertas, Passeig d'Isabel 11, 14   Tel: 319 3033 ££
A good traditional restaurant, established mid-19th century,
specialised in Catalan cuisine. Excellent for seafood and rice
dishes.

Can Sole, Sant Carlos 4   Tel: 319 5012 ££
Nearing its centenary, a charming old tavern restaurant with
excellent seafood.
Closed Sat night, Sun, first two weeks of Feb and first two
weeks of Sep.

El Salmonete, Cárrer Vinaroz   Tel: 319 5032 ££
At the far end of Barceloneta, special for seafood. Order a
delicious paella, and eat on the beach.

Planet Hollywood, Marina 19-21, Centro Comercial Marina
Village.   Tel: 221 1111.

BARCELONA

In Diagonal area – Metro: Diagonal. Numerous restaurants of all types are grouped close around Plaça de Francesc Macia and near Hotels Wilson, Presidente and Condado.

Reno, Tuset 27   Tel: 200 9129 £££
Elegant, serving excellent French and Catalan food.
La Dorada, Travesera de Gràcia 44   Tel: 200 6322 £££
Andalusian cuisine, specialising in seafood and stews.
La Oca, Plaça de Francesc Macia   Tel: 321 7641 ££
In the heart of the business centre, this restaurant is open all day, from 7.30 a.m. till midnight.
Tramonti, Diagonal 501   Tel: 250 1535 ££
Possibly the best Italian restaurant in Barcelona, with a superb range of pastas and cheeses.
Near to Plaça Francesc Macia. Closed in August.
Solera Gallega, Paris 176   Tel: 322 9140 ££
Friendly atmosphere. Very good for seafood. Expensive but good quality.
El Pa Torrat, Santalo 68   Tel: 209 1779 ££
In front of Galvany Market, a good restaurant for Catalan food.
Flash Flash, La Granada 25   Tel: 237 0990 £
A favourite haunt of Barcelonans, serving and incredible range of omelettes and fresh salads. Open till 1.30 a.m.

Other districts
La Orotava, Consell de Cent 335   Tel: 302 3128 £££
An exquisite jet-set restaurant, with superb quality and service, specialising in game and seafood. Evening meals only. Very expensive. Closed Sunday.
Metro: Passeig de Gràcia.
El Dorado Petit, Dolors Monserda 51   Tel: 204 5153 £££
One of Barcelona's finest restaurants, set in a private villa. Excellent cuisine, both nouvelle and traditional. Memorable fish dishes. Reservation essential.
Metro: Reina Elisenda - end of line on northern outskirts.
Azulete, Via Augusta 281   Tel: 203 5943 £££
A beautiful restaurant set in an old conservatory. Cooking is a choice of Catalan, French and Italian with some interesting and inventive traditional and new dishes. Closed Sat lunch, Sun, fiestas and first two weeks of August.
Metro: Les Tres Torres
Hostal Sant Jordi, Travessera de Dalt 123
Catalan and French cuisine of a very high standard. Closed Sun evenings and August.   Tel: 213 1037 ££
Metro: Lesseps
Pa i Trago, Parlament 41   Tel: 241 1320 ££
Typical Catalan cuisine, specialising in grills. Closed: mon and from 24 July to 24 Aug.
Metro: Poble Sec

La Clara d'Ou, Gran Via C.C. 442   Tel: 325 2931 ££
Another interesting Catalan restaurant. Try their black rice speciality. Closed holiday evenings and Monday; Holy Week and 15 days in August.
Metro: Rocafort

El Caballito Blanco, Mallorca 196   Tel: 253 1033 £
Very popular restaurant with simple cooking and a good variety of cheeses. Closed Sun evenings, Mon and August.
Metro: Provenca

3.10 Nightlife in Barcelona

Barcelona's nightlife is comparable to most major European cities'. Whether you want music from classics to jazz, a nightclub, disco or bar, Barcelona can provide something for every night of your stay.

Concerts
Barcelona rivals Madrid for classical music, opera and ballet. Check on programmes given by the Barcelona Municipal Orchestra and other groups, based on the **Palau de la Música Catalana** or on the new **Auditorium** on the Plaça de les Arts (Metro: Marina). Evening concerts most often start at 21 hrs. Some concerts are given on Sunday mornings. Location of the concert hall is Amadeu Vives 1, just off the Via Laietana. Metro: Jaume 1.

    Box office hours are: Mon-Fri 11-13 & 17-20 hrs; Sat 17-20 hrs. On the day, tickets are available from 17 hrs onwards.

Opera
The **Gran Teatre del Liceu** – a mid-19th century building located midway along the Rambla – was one of Europe's great opera theatres, with capacity for 3500 audience. Regrettably it burnt down in 1994, but is now being reconstructed in a similar style and decoration. Hopefully it will reopen in 1997. Meanwhile opera is staged occasionally at the Palau Música Catalana (Tel: 268 1000) or at the Teatro Victoria on Avda. Paral-lel. (Tel: 412 3532).

Some bars to sample
Dry Martini, Paris 102 – A trendy cocktail lounge. Closed Sun and last two weeks of August.
Ideal Cocktail Bar, Aribau 89 – Closed Sun and last two weeks of August.
Merbeyer, Plaça Dr. Andreu – Open till 3 a.m. Closed Sun.
Els Quatre Gats, Montsió 5 – still retains the turn-of-century atmosphere of Picasso and his friends, a meeting-place for fervent discussion till 2 a.m.

BARCELONA

La Fira, Provenca 171 – a bar that doubles as a museum of old-time fairground rides.
(Metro: Diagonal/Provenca)

Champagne Bars

Brut, Trompetas 3 – popular with the after-theatre crowd.
La Folie, Bailen 169 – good atmosphere and pleasant decor.
La Xampaneria, Provenca 236 – the first champagne bar, and still the best, with elegant service.

Discos

Studio 54, Paral-lel 64. Excellent shows and lots of excitement. Open Fri, Sat & Sun only. Metro: Paral-lel.
Fibra Optica, Beethoven 9. Open 18-21.30 and 23.30-05 hrs.
Otto Zutz, Lincoln 15. Open 22-02 hrs, and then becomes a members-only club. A bit weird, with all-black decor.

Jazz Cafés

Abraxas Jazz Auditorium, Gelabert 26
Live and recorded music, mostly jazz. Closed Mon and August.
La Cora del Drac, Tuset 30 (off La Diagonal)
Excellent live music. Closed Sun.

Flamenco

Barcelona is not the best place for flamenco, which is an Andalusian creation. But there are some flamenco shows which can compare. At most establishments you can choose to arrive for the show only with drink included; or take an inclusive dinner and show deal.

Andalucia, Rambla 27   Tel: 302 2009
Dinner from 20.30-22 hrs, followed at 22.30 hrs by flamenco and Spanish dancing until midnight.

Cordobes, Rambla 35   Tel: 317 6653
Show from 22-23.30 & 23.30-01.30 hrs.

Los Tarantos, Pl. Reial 17   Tel: 317 8098
Good flamenco shows, three times a night between 22 and 05 hrs.

El Patio Andaluz, Aribau 242   Tel: 209 3524
From 22-24 hrs.

Music-Hall

Belle Epoque, Muntaner 246   Tel: 209 7385
Excellent shows, daily except Sunday, at 23.30 hrs. Prices - drink included – are somewhat higher on Fri & Sat.

Stage show with dinner

Scala Barcelona, Passeig de Sant Joan 47   Tel: 232 6363
Leading nightclub with two lavish international shows including ballet and variety acts. Spanish dancing is normally part of the show during the summer season. Dinner, dancing and show from 20.15 hrs; show and a drink from 00.15 hrs. Gentlemen should wear tie and jacket.

Barcelona by Night

Agencies offer varied packages of transport with flamenco show or Scala Barcelona, with dinner and/or a drink included. Ask your tour rep for details.

Poble Espanyol

For widest possible choice of entertainment, spend an evening at Poble Espanyol on Montjuïc. The Spanish Village features around 40 varied establishments including music bars, jazz cellars, discos, and restaurants with shows. The village is open daily until the small hours, but is especially lively at weekends.

Tablao de Carmen

At the Poble Espanyol features Andalusian cuisine, then flamenco at 23 hrs and at 00.45 hrs.

Barrio Chino

The Barrio Chino area is not recommended for a romantic midnight stroll. This famed port area has declined in social esteem, and ladies of the town have relocated. The local daily newspaper La Vanguardia has dozens of phone numbers and addresses among the small-ads, classified as Relax, or Estetica, or Relaciones.

3.11 At your service in Barcelona

Banks & Exchange Bureaux

Outside of normal bank and travel-agency hours, the airport exchange office is open 7-23 hrs daily. At Central-Sants railway station, an exchange office is open 8-20 hrs daily; or until 22 hrs during summer. Sunday opening during summer is 8-14 and 16-22 hrs.

Post Office & Telephone

Local post offices are open 9-14 hrs Mon-Fri, and some open in the afternoon. The main post office in Plaça d'Antoni Lopez (at bottom of Via Laietana by the harbour) is open Mon-Fri 9-21 and Sat 9-14 hrs.
Barcelona phone numbers have seven digits. The area code is 93, but dial 34-3 when calling from outside Spain.

BARCELONA

Emergency telephone numbers
Police 091 or 092
Doctor 212 8585
Ambulance 300 2020

Other phone numbers and addresses
Police: during summer from July 1, English-speaking police
are on duty 24 hours a day at Rambla 43. Tel: 317 7020.
The Airport: Tel 370 1011

Lost Property
City Hall Tel: 301 3923

Medical
Emergency hospital services are operated by:
The Hospital of Sant Pau, Av. S. Antoni María Claret 167.
Tel: 347 3133.
Hospital Clinic, Casanova 143. Tel: 323 1414.
Red Cross Hospital, Dos de Maig 301. Tel: 235 9300.

Consulates
British: Av. Diagonal 477 Tel: 322 2151
American: Via Laietana 33 Tel: 319 9550
Canadian: Via Augusta 125 Tel: 209 0634
Irish: Gran Via Carles 111, 94 Tel: 330 9652
South Africa: Gran Via C.C. 634 Tel: 318 0797

Tourist Information
From July to September, young information officers work in
pairs in the streets of the historic centre – the Gothic Quarter
and the Ramblas. Known as "Red Jackets" they wear red
and white uniforms, and have an information badge. Duty
hours are 9-21 hrs.

Information is also available from Tourist Board offices at:

Gothic Quarter – Plaça Sant Jaume   Tel: 318 2525
Barcelona Harbour – Moll de la Fusta, near *Santa María*
replica   Tel: 310 3716
Open: 15 June to 30 Sep 08-20 hrs. Otherwise 9-15 hrs.
Central Station Barcelona-Sants – Vestibule
Open: 8-20 hrs.   Tel: 410 2594
Barcelona Trade Fair – Plaça de l'Univers
Open: 10-20 hrs during Trade Fairs.   Tel: 325 5235
Barcelona Airport – International arrivals Tel: 325 5829
Open: Mon-Sat 09.30-20 hrs. 15 June till 15 Sep also on
Sundays 9-15 hrs.
Catalonia Information - Gran Via C.C. 658
Open: Mon-Fri 9-19 hrs. Sat 9-14 hrs.   Tel: 301 7443

Chapter Four

Seville

4.1 Discover Seville

For six months during 1992, Seville held the world stage as the setting for Expo '92. The site was chosen because of Seville's close connection with the story of Christopher Columbus, for whom 1992 marked the 500th anniversary of the discovery of the New World. Appropriately the theme of this great international show was 'Discovery'.

As spin-off from all the TV and press coverage, millions of people around the world likewise made a discovery – that Seville itself is worth a special journey to explore its rich history from the Golden Age of Spain.

The great prosperity of Seville dates from 1503, when the city was granted the monopoly of all trade with the Americas. It was literally a Golden Age, with cargoes of treasure being unloaded on the quayside, where it was stored in the Torre del Oro – the Tower of Gold – for safe keeping. That building is still in good shape, housing a small Maritime Museum. Seville itself was far enough up the Guadalquivir River to escape the attentions of Drake and Raleigh.

With such riches, Seville could afford splendid churches, monasteries and public buildings, while spacious mansions housed the wealthy and the aristocratic. Artists found ample demand for their works, both religious and secular.

Later, when the government of Spain was centralized in Madrid, the income from South America gradually fell away, and Seville could only dream of past glories. Seville kept its role as an Andalusian centre, while losing its function as the undisputed gateway to Latin America. In the 19th century, the Industrial Revolution never reached that far south.

Just as the Olympics triggered new construction in Barcelona, the holding of Expo '92 sparked a massive investment in Seville's infrastructure, designed to help the city leap into the 20th century. Seville's entire road system has been re-modelled, with construction of more than 30 miles of ring roads and avenues. Seven new bridges over the Guadalquivir river have improved movement of traffic through and around the city, which formerly had only four bridges.

SEVILLE

Andalusia is now completely linked into the European motorway network. Travelling from Madrid to Seville is much easier and shorter along the Andalusia Motorway. The Seville-Granada-Baza Motorway connects with the Mediterranean seaboard motorway system in Alicante. Motorists can reach Seville from virtually anywhere in continental Europe without coming off the dual carriageway.

In a 15th-century monastery on Cartuja Island in the Guadalquivir River, Columbus discussed plans for his great voyages of discovery. For Columbus and his family, the monastery was an occasional lodging and a permanent strongroom deposit for his mass of papers and legal documents. After his death he was buried for 27 years in a monastery chapel. His brother and his son were also buried in the monastery, which effectively served as a provisional family vault.

The renovated monastery was the focal point of Expo '92, and is preserved as a national monument. But possibly more important for the future of Seville, many of the fairground installations are now being used as the nucleus of a Science Park to create one of the world's best equipped high-tech zones. Today's dream is to convert Andalusia into a European California, blessed with blue skies and 21st-century technology, linked to an appealing lifestyle.

Traditionally Seville is a city of colourful atmosphere. Even today, Seville is probably best known for its dazzling fiestas. Seville annually hosts over a million people during the six days and nights of the April Fair, when the whole city erupts into a flamboyant fairground of horse and carriage parades, fireworks, bullfights and dancing.

The entire world of Spanish song and dance is available year-round in Seville – flamenco guitar and song, Spanish pop-rock and light music. Along with the city's great historical background, Seville has great Citybreak appeal. Read on!

4.2 Arrival & Public Transport

By taxi from airport to the city centre costs between 1,500-1,800 ptas, and takes 15-20 minutes. Iberia, Spain's national airline, operates a Madrid-Seville service which enables visitors in Madrid to make a brief excursion to Seville.

Equally competitive in time – Madrid city centre to Seville centre – is a high-speed 150-mph rail service which does the journey in 2 hours 30 minutes, compared with the previous 6 hours. The modernized Santa Justa station has been resited to permit the opening of a new stretch of promenade alongside the Guadalquivir River. The river itself has been rerouted to follow its original course through Seville.

Linkage with the Costa del Sol motorway permits fast access to Seville from any of the coastal resorts.

City Transport

Seville's sightseeing highlights are mostly within easy walking distance of the Cathedral. If your hotel is not quite so handy, ask the front desk for bus directions to the centre.

On a short stay, with distances relatively small, taxis will not dig deep into your budget, but will certainly save sightseeing time. Radio Taxis, phone: 458 0000; 462 2222; or 435 9835.

More expensive are the tourist horse-carriage rides that cost about 4,000 ptas for under an hour. Shared among 4 or 5 passengers, the price sounds more reasonable. Agree the fare and route before embarcation. Carriage ranks are located in front of the Cathedral, and at Plaza de España.

4.3 Get your bearings

Quite simply, start at the Cathedral Square – the Plaza del Triunfo. This is a delightful location in itself, where shallow steps around a commemorative column make an informal meeting place for the young. There are stone benches where the more elderly can take the sun and gossip, while carriages drawn by white horses wait for passengers.

Here you are surrounded by the prime sightseeing highlights: the Cathedral and its landmark Giralda bell-tower; the Alcázar palace and gardens; the Santa Cruz quarter. There's the facade of the Bishop's Palace to admire, and the rather stern Lonja which houses the Archives of the Indies.

From this central location, most of the other sites are within a few minutes' walk – westwards to the Charity Hospital, Golden Tower and the river promenade; south-east to the old Tobacco Factory which is now part of Seville University, and thence to Plaza de España and the María Luisa Park.

North of the Cathedral are spread the main shopping streets. For other sightseeing targets in that direction – like the House of Pilatus, the Macarena Basilica and the Museum of Fine Arts – just save your legs and take a short taxi-ride.

Like most ancient cities, Seville was originally fortified. A few stretches of the wall still remain from the 12th century – principally by the Macarena Gate which has been recently renovated.

Otherwise the main line of the city wall is marked by the inner ring road which then loops round the Alcázar walls and finishes at the Golden Tower.

Apart from the María Luisa Park and its adjoining sites, virtually everything worth your time on a short City Break is contained within that original line of city walls.

Whenever you lose your bearings, especially in the maze-like Santa Cruz quarter, just search the skyline for that ever-helpful landmark, the Giralda.

SEVILLE

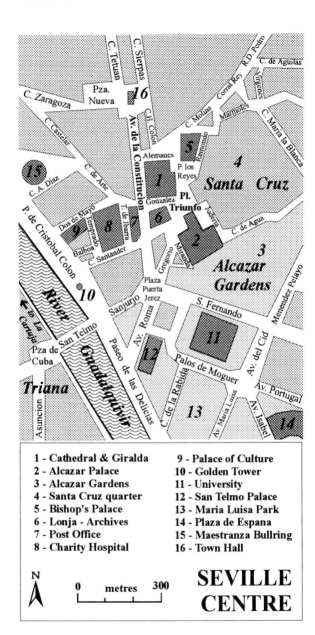

1 - Cathedral & Giralda
2 - Alcazar Palace
3 - Alcazar Gardens
4 - Santa Cruz quarter
5 - Bishop's Palace
6 - Lonja - Archives
7 - Post Office
8 - Charity Hospital
9 - Palace of Culture
10 - Golden Tower
11 - University
12 - San Telmo Palace
13 - Maria Luisa Park
14 - Plaza de Espana
15 - Maestranza Bullring
16 - Town Hall

N

0   metres   300

SEVILLE
CENTRE

4.4 Basic Seville

Seville has at least two or three days' potential city sightseeing to delight even the most hurried traveller. Here's a basic check-list for enjoyment of a brief stay.

(1) Go strolling through the Santa Cruz district for a taste of romantic travel-poster Seville. *See map, fig. 4.*
(2) Visit the Cathedral, one of the world's most impressive. *See map, fig. 1.*
(3) Explore the Moorish style Alcázar. *See map, fig. 2.*
(4) Climb the 12th century Giralda minaret for a bird's-eye view of the city.
(5) Go to the Basilica of La Macarena, where costumes, images and floats for the famed Holy Week are displayed.
(6) Take a horse-carriage ride from the Cathedral to the Plaza de España *(see map, fig. 14)* for old-time Seville.
(7) Visit the María Luisa park, and the Museum of Folk Arts and Costumes. *See map, fig. 13.* Go at weekend, when Spanish families are enjoying the air with their children.
(8) Explore the riverside promenade, and take an hour's sightseeing boat ride from the Torre del Oro where 16th-century cargoes of gold were unloaded. *See map, fig. 10.*
(9) Enjoy an evening at a flamenco show.
(10) Check the music programmes and hope to get tickets for a performance at the Maestranza Theatre. *See map, fig. 9.*

The Cathedral

Tourist visits to the Cathedral are permitted 10.30-13 and 16-18.30 hrs in summer; 10.30-13 and 15.30-17.30 hrs in winter. *See map, fig. 1.*

The Cathedral is the focal point of the city's main monuments. Originally the Great Mosque of Seville stood here, built by 12th-century Moors on the site of a Visigoth church. After the Moors were driven out in 1248, the mosque was converted to Christianity. It was then demolished from 1401, to be replaced by the present-day building – the third largest church in the world, after St. Peter's in Rome and St. Paul's in London.

According to a proudly-displayed certificate from the Guinness Book of Records, it's the Cathedral with the world's largest interior – 126 metres long, 83 metres wide, 30 metres high. Certainly it rates as the world's largest Gothic building. Its enormous size does not become apparent until you go inside and feel dwarfed.

Completed by 1507, the Cathedral has five large Gothic naves and varied additions in Renaissance and Baroque styles. The 45 chapels formerly belonged to aristocratic families for their private use. They are richly decorated mini art galleries, with works by Murillo, Zurbarán and Goya.

SEVILLE

Most outstanding is the Royal Chapel, a masterpiece completed 1575 in the silver-work style called Plateresque (from the Spanish word *plata*, meaning silver). The Royal Chapel was purpose-built for the Spanish kings, and several are buried here. At the foot of the altar is the silver tomb of the embalmed Saint Fernando the Conqueror – the king who recaptured Seville. On top of the 18th-century grille is a bronze equestrian figure of Saint Fernando receiving the city keys after he defeated the Moors.

At the altar is La Virgen de los Reyes – the Madonna of the Kings – a gift from King Louis IX of France to Fernando. She is Seville's patron saint, greatly venerated. On the left is the tomb of Alfonso the Wise, the son of Fernando; and on the right is Fernando's wife, Beatrice of Swabia. In the crypt below the altar is the coffin of King Pedro the Cruel. Numerous Spanish kings gaze down from the Renaissance dome.

But the Cathedral's greatest highlight is the main altar - the largest and richest reredos in all Europe. Divided into 45 tableaux, it contains 1080 figures of gilded wood representing the lives of Jesus and Mary. Rated among the finest works of Spanish sculpture, its artistic value is far greater than the cash value of all the gold. Consider the masterly use of perspective, for instance. The figures at the top are four times larger than those lower down; but from ground level they all appear to be the same size. In the lower part is the Madonna called Santa María de la Cede, to whom the Cathedral is dedicated.

The Chapel of La Virgen de La Antigua contains a 14th-century Madonna, greatly revered by Spanish sailors and navigators. Columbus came here to pray before departing on a new trip. This chapel is used only once a year – on 12 October, the anniversary of the discovery of America. The chapel was refurbished for the 500th anniversary, at a cost of £650,000.

Columbus died in Valladolid and was originally buried at La Cartuja Monastery, the site of Expo '92. But from 1536 the bones of Columbus continued their travels. In 1544 they arrived in Santo Domingo, the capital of Hispaniola (today's Dominican Republic). When Spain lost that colony, Columbus was possibly reburied in Cuba. Then maybe he came back to Seville for interment in the cathedral.

However, there were probably mix-ups in the itinerary, bones are easily confused, and Santo Domingo is among the dozen or more cities which still claim possession.

Seville's burial monument to Columbus was installed early this century. Figures carrying the coffin represent the four kingdoms of Spain at the time of his voyage – León, Castille, Navarre and Aragón.

There are some bones inside, but whose?

The cathedral treasury is located in the Main Sacristy, heavily decorated in Plateresque style: silver everywhere. Look at the monstrance made with 300 kilos of the metal.

Alongside the Cathedral is the Patio de los Oranjos. This Orange Tree Courtyard with its still-functioning irrigation system, together with the Giralda, is all that remains of the original mosque. The basin of the central fountain is even older – a survival from Visigoth times.

Also in this historic location is the Columbus Library – a 3,000-volume collection donated by the Admiral's son and including original Columbus manuscripts and documents.

The Giralda

The cathedral belfry which dominates the skyline of central Seville was originally a mosque minaret built in 1184 on a Roman foundation. The basic pattern follows that of its Moroccan twins in Marrakech and Rabat, with superb decorative brickwork.

In 1568 the minaret was finally re-shaped by adding the present 25-bell tower, topped by a statue of Faith which turns with the wind. Hence the name of *Giraldillo*, meaning weathervane. A copy of the Faith weathervane gathers dust in a corner of the Cathedral.

Open daily 11-17 hrs; Sun & hols 11-13 hrs. Entrance: 300 ptas. There are no steps to climb to the 308-ft summit – just a steep incline, up which VIPs formerly rode on horseback.

The Alcázar

The Moorish citadel is the sumptuous highspot of Seville's sightseeing circuit. From 712 AD the Arab conquerors laid out the basic ground-plan of fortress walls, palace buildings and gardens. But the best parts of today's palace were built during the reign of Pedro the Cruel (1350-1369), who lived here with his mistress María de Padilla.

He sent for Moorish craftsmen from Granada and Toledo, and commanded a five-star luxury palace. The style is Mudéjar – basically a mixture of Arabian Nights' fantasy with Christian symbols. The favourite decoration is stucco, a combination of plaster and powdered alabaster.

Entrance through the Lion Gate leads into a delightful garden with softly rustling fountains, and thence to the Patio de la Monteria. Ahead is the superb facade of Peter the Cruel's palace. To the right is an audience hall where Queen Isabella welcomed Columbus when he returned from his second voyage. Many other great journeys of discovery were planned here, such as those by Balboa and Magellan.

Go into Peter the Cruel's palace through the large rectangular door, and everything from there onwards is curved. Central to the palace layout is the very beautiful and elaborate Maidens' Patio, where palace life revolved. The name

SEVILLE

possibly derives from the Moorish Kings' custom of demanding an annual tribute of a hundred Christian virgins.

Opening out from this courtyard are two large halls which lead off to varied apartments, living rooms and bedrooms, all richly decorated. Rivalling anything in Granada is the Ambassador's Hall with a huge cedar-wood door, tiles, delicate stucco and a half-orange domed ceiling, all in excellent condition. Discreet lighting helps bring out the details sharply. The ensemble is breathtaking.

Adjoining the main palace are the apartments of Charles V, added in 16th century for his wedding to Isabel of Portugal. A dozen large tapestries depict his conquest of Tunisia.

The next main stop is for a large goldfish pond that overlooks the peaceful Gardens, thick with orange and lemon trees, date palms, neatly clipped hedges, myrtle bushes and prickly pear. It's just like a fertile corner of Morocco. Be sure to leave time to stroll around! *See map, fig. 3.*
Open: Tue-Sat 10.30-18 hrs; Sun & hols 10-14 hrs. Closed Mon. Entrance: 600 ptas.

Santa Cruz Quarter

In medieval times this was a Jewish district. After expulsion of the Jews, the ghetto was renamed Santa Cruz – Holy Cross – and the 13th-century synagogue became the church of Santa María la Blanca. Only a minute's walk from the royal palace and the cathedral, Santa Cruz became an up-market residential area for the nobility. *See map, fig. 4.* Every building is beautifully preserved.

The best way to explore Santa Cruz is to wander at random, not attempting any set itinerary. Every little street and plaza has its charm. Balconies drip with flowers, windows are barred with wrought-iron grilles, and walls gleam with whitewash, or are coloured green or yellow-ochre.

There are decorative tiles everywhere, and heavily studded timbered doors. Peek in through open passages, and you get views into delightful shaded patios or courtyards.

All along the streets are Seville-orange trees, good for marmalade not for breakfast juice. With their golden fruit they make superb colour pictures. Springtime gives added pleasure from the fragrance of the blossom. Around every corner is another stage set for romantic opera, or the model for a travel poster.

Plaza de España and María Luisa Park

In 1929 an Ibero-American Exhibition was held in Seville, with participation of Latin American countries. The purpose-built venue for that Exhibition – the curved colonnade of the Plaza de España – is a highlight of today's sightseeing.

The scene in Plaza de España *(see map, fig. 14)* is almost impossibly romantic. The semi-circular colonnade is lined with painted tiles that depict maps and historical scenes from all the provinces of Spain. In the foreground is a boating circuit with graceful curved bridges of fanciful design. Every balustrade is covered in ceramics.

Flocks of white doves pose for their pictures, while a succession of tourist horse-carriages halt in front of the main entrance. There is colour everywhere.

Facing the Plaza de España is the María Luisa Park, crammed with exotic trees – palms, bananas and chestnuts, orange, pecan and strawberry trees. *See map, fig. 13.* Varied statues are dedicated to poets and playwrights, and also to Princess María Luisa who donated this half of her royal palace garden to the public.

Macarena Basilica

If you cannot make Seville during its world-famed Holy Week, next best thing is to visit the Macarena Basilica. Located at one of the old city gates – Puerta de la Macarena – the Basilica is famed for its La Macarena Madonna, the most popular participant in the Holy Week processions. The Basilica is relatively new, completed in 1949. The original church was burnt down in 1936 during the Spanish Civil War, but the 17th-century baroque Madonna and other figures were kept hidden and escaped damage.

La Macarena is famous throughout Spain and in all South American countries, especially Mexico and Columbia. She is also known as Madonna of the Bullfighters. Originally, Seville's matadors came here on bullfight days, to pray in front of the Madonna before braving the bulls. Now they pray in a small chapel at the bullring itself. Obviously the prayers work. Only one bullfighter has been killed in the Maestranza bullring since its foundation in 1758.

The Macarena Basilica virtually doubles as a museum, exhibiting all the details of Seville's renowned Holy Week processions. There are 56 Brotherhoods, based on different churches around Seville. During Holy Week seven or eight processions every day take a different route to the Cathedral and back.

Each procession is led by two extremely heavy floats called *pasos*, derived from a Latin word meaning 'to suffer'. The first float represents a scene from the Passion of Christ; the second is always a Madonna, crying. Each 3-ton float is painfully carried from underneath its canopy by 48 men on the 12-hour journey to and from the Cathedral. Hooded penitents follow the floats.

The Macarena Basilica exhibits the Madonna in her green and white robes, the floats, and figures which represent the episode when Pilate is about to wash his hands. These images are important masterpieces made by leading sculptors in the 17th and 18th century.

SEVILLE

Also in the Treasury are bullfighter costumes donated by grateful Sevillian matadors; display cases of jewelry given by admirers in Seville and South America; even a model Rolls-Royce in gold.

There are richly-embroidered mantles of the Madonna, requiring a magnifying glass to appreciate the delicacy of the needlework. An embroidered mantle of this quality takes five or six women working together at least five years.

Open: 9.30-12 & 17-20 hrs.

Casa de Pilatos – Pilate's House – Plaza de Pilatos

Why that name? There are various theories, but it seems that the building was intended as a copy of Pontius Pilate's house in Jerusalem. The aristocratic builder of this mainly 16th-century palace, Fadrique de Ribera, had visited Jerusalem and the south of Italy. He returned, to put his lavish ideas into effect.

Typical of Andalusia, the family lived on the upper floor in the winter, and on the lower part in summer around the patios. All rooms around the patio were decorated with cool materials like ceramics and marble. When the present owners are in Seville they live only upstairs. So the upper part is normally closed to visitors.

The lower floor is Mudéjar style – not pure Moroccan, but a mixture of Arabic flavoured with Christian motifs: built by Moorish craftsmen for a Christian owner. The very fine stucco work is well preserved. The upper gallery, added later, is Renaissance style.

Most of the 16th-century Renaissance statuary was brought back by Ribera from southern Italy. Two figures portray Minerva and Ceres – wisdom and agriculture. The medallions represent Roman emperors. There are also some genuine Roman statues, trophies from Itálica – the former Roman base just north of Seville.

In the garden are all the most typical trees of Seville – oranges and lemons, fig trees, magnolia, palm and jacaranda. Springtime offers a fantastic flowering of yellow jasmine and bougainvillea.

Around the cedar-wood doors – made from timber imported from Lebanon – are inscriptions from the Koran, and a listing of important happenings. An estimated 500,000 tiles were used in the palace decoration, with some 120 different designs. Finally, admire the finest main staircase in Seville: decorated in wood, stucco in the middle, and all the lower part covered with tiles. Above is a half-orange dome to rival a similar construction in the Ambassador Room at the Alcázar. It all gives a good idea of the aristocratic life-style during the Golden Age of Seville.

Open: 9-13 & 15-19 hrs in summer; 9-13 & 15-18 hrs in winter. Entrance: 500 ptas.

4.5 Other sights in Seville

In two or three days you cannot expect to see much more than Basic Seville, described in the previous section. If you can squeeze another day or two into your itinerary, here's a selection of other sights to consider.

Cartuja Monastery

During 1992 the monastery buildings were the focal point of Expo, basking in the glory of their close connection with the Columbus saga. After Expo, the completely refurbished monastery has become a regular part of the sightseeing circuit, in contrast to its chequered career of the past 200 years. Entrance 300 ptas.

In 1835, during the Carlist Wars, church lands were nationalized and sold off. The monastery of La Cartuja was closed, and the monks expelled. In 1838 the buildings were leased to an English industrialist, Charles Pickman of Liverpool, for establishment of a high-quality pottery works.

The agreement was that the original monastery structure should remain. The Columbus chapel and the church were converted by Pickman as a warehouse for raw materials and finished products. A little steam train took the wares from the factory to the river, for shipment.

Pickman introduced the style of bottle ovens which were a key part of Stoke-on-Trent's technical revolution in the firing of pottery.

At its peak, the factory employed 1200 workers. Even today, every Spanish bride dreams of having a set of La Cartuja tableware as a wedding present.

After 140 years the company moved to other premises in Seville, while La Cartuja and its grounds became a national monument owned by the Andalusian regional government. The original potbank has been restored, as an industrial heritage reminder of 19th-century technology.

Take a riverside walk

Northwards from María Luisa Park a riverside promenade has now been extended to way past Cartuja Island. Several buildings of sightseeing interest are closely grouped: the Torre del Oro (Golden Tower), the Hospital de la Caridad (Charity Hospital), the Maestranza Bullring, and the new Maestranza Opera House which was inaugurated in May 1991. *See map, figs. 10, 8, 9 and 15.*

Just concentrating on that key area, it's worth making a circuit by crossing the river on the San Telmo and the Isabel II bridges, to get a better panoramic view of central Seville's skyline.

Numerous bars, discos and restaurants are a popular feature of the Triana side of the river.

SEVILLE

Torre del Oro – Tower of Gold – Paseo de Colon

The greatest prosperity of Seville came from 1503 onwards, when the city was granted monopoly of all trade with the Americas. It was literally a Golden Age, when cargoes of tobacco, cocoa beans and gold were unloaded on the quayside beside the 12-sided Torre del Oro. *See map, fig. 10.*

The Torre del Oro was used as a temporary storage place for gold from the New World. The building was certainly strong enough for a Fort Knox role, having been built in 1220 by the Moors as part of the city fortifications.

A defensive chain crossed the river to a similar Silver Tower on the Triana side, to hinder the passage of any invading fleet.

From the broad promenade there are good views across the river, where small boats can be hired. Alongside the Tower, cruise boats offer day or night trips.

The Torre del Oro is still in good shape, housing a tiny Maritime Museum – maps, ancient navigation instruments and documents relating to the naval history of Seville and its river.

Open: Tue-Fri 10-14; Sat-Sun 10-13 hrs.   Tel: 422 2419

Hospital de la Caridad – Calle Temprado

The Charity Hospital *(see map, fig. 8)* is located just behind the Maestranza Opera House, newly built on Núñez de Balboa square. By coincidence there's a close connection between Grand Opera and the history of the Charity Hospital.

According to legend, a wealthy and licentious character called Don Miguel de Mañara was returning from another wild orgy when he had a vision of a burial procession carrying his own corpse.

In a sudden fit of repentance he turned to religion, joined a Charity Brotherhood devoted to the burial of criminals and the destitute, and in 1676 opened this hospital for the aged and penniless.

The story was picked up by Byron for his *Don Juan* poem, and by Mozart for *Don Giovanni*.

The Charity Hospital itself is used as an alms-house, with 45 aged male residents who enjoy the tranquility of the patio with its Flemish tiles.

For the adjoining church, Don Miguel commissioned Murillo to paint a dozen masterpieces designed to show an Exemplary Christian Life founded on Charity. The pictures are rated among Murillo's finest works.

Four of the paintings were liberated by Napoleon's army in 1810 and now hang in London, New York, Ottawa and St. Petersburg. There are two famous 'death' pictures by Valdés Leal – one representing a decomposing bishop rotting among maggots. Certainly worth a visit!

Open: Mon-Sat 10-13 and 15.30-18 hrs.

Maestranza Bullring – Paseo Colón 12   Tel: 422 4577.
The bullfight season begins throughout the week of April
Fair and continues most Sundays until September. This
bullring, built 1760, is the most prestigious in Spain and has
a star role in *Carmen*. Other events are sometimes held here,
such as equestrian displays on Saturdays. *See map, fig. 15.*

In the ring, the traditional golden-yellow sand called
albero is quarried in Seville province. Many park walks also
are covered in the sand, while innumerable buildings echo
this same colour, characteristic of the city.

The bullring and a bullfighting museum can be visited on
non-bullfight days, but check times first. Entrance 250 ptas.

The Tobacco Factory
For more memories of *Carmen*, you can't help noticing the
former Tobacco Factory, the second largest building in Spain
after El Escorial. Built for the Tabacalera tobacco monopoly
in 1751, the gigantic building occupying an entire city block
just south of the Alcázar Gardens is now used by Seville
University. Laughing gipsy tobacco girls with carnations in
their teeth are replaced by students on mopeds.

This very solid building needs repainting, but otherwise is
in good shape. *See map, fig. 11.*

4.6 Museums and galleries

Fine Arts Museum, Plaza del Museo 9   Tel: 422 0790
Occupying a former convent, the Museum is rated in Spain
as the second richest art gallery after the Prado. It features a
major collection of works especially by Murillo, Zurbarán
and Valdés Leal, but also canvases by Velázquez, El Greco,
Rubens, Tiziano and Goya.

All this artistic wealth is not surprising. The riches from
Seville's Golden Age was reflected in the city's attraction to
the leading artists of the day. Velásquez was born in Seville,
though he afterwards moved to Madrid. Zurbarán flourished
in Seville, and here Murillo was born and worked. The
museum also contains a wide assortment of sculptures, pottery, furniture, embroidery and gold pieces.
Open: probably 10-14 hrs but check first whether restoration
work has been completed.

Archaeological Museum, María Luisa Park Tel: 423 2401
Sited in a neo-Renaissance pavilion built in 1919, this well-
endowed museum is among the most important in Spain. Its
supreme exhibit is the Carambolo Treasure comprising 21
solid-gold items dating from 6th century BC. Numerous
marble statues and mosaics have come from the Roman site
of Itálica. Open: 10-13 hrs. Closed: Mon and holidays.

SEVILLE

Contemporary Art Museum, S. Tomas 1   Tel: 421 5830
This gallery is right next door to the former Loja which has
been converted into the Archives of the Indies. It offers a
cross-section of 20th-century Spanish painting and sculpture.
Open: Tue-Fri 10-19 hrs; Sat-Sun 10-14 hrs. Closed Mon.
Entrance: free for citizens of European Community.

Museum of Folk Arts and Popular Customs
Plaza de América, María Luisa Park   Tel: 423 2576
Top marks for a wide range of interest! On the first floor is
an attractive display of turn-of-the-century posters publicizing
Holy Week and the Seville Fair. Each poster is worth a
colour photograph in itself.

Then there's all kinds of costume display, and accessories
such as mantillas, fans and umbrellas. A collection of popular musical instruments includes the obvious drums and flutes
as used on festive occasions; and also other folk instruments
such as a kind of rustic drum called a zambomba.

Rural industries and trades are well presented, with authentic workshops – a bakery, a blacksmith's, tanner's shop
and a pottery. Don't miss this museum for the best overview
of the traditional Andalusian life-style! It's delightful to see
some of the local villagers, walking round and exclaiming
with pleasure as they see items familiar to their childhood.
Open: 10-14.30 hrs Tue-Sun. Entrance: free.

The Indies Archives (Archivo General de Indias)
Av. de la Constitución   Tel: 421 1234
Located between the Cathedral and the Alcázar, this late
16th-century Renaissance building houses around 38,000
documents relating to discoveries and conquests in the New
World from the 15th to 19th century. Among the treasures
are Christopher Columbus' diary, the first maps of colonial
settlements, and the autographs of Magellan and Cortes.
Open: 10-13 hrs.

4.7 Take a trip

Seville offers more than enough interest to keep a visitor
well occupied for several days. But if you want to take a
trip, here are three suggestions.

Down the river
Pleasure cruises along the Guadalquivir operate from the
Torre del Oro landing stage. A popular one-hour journey is
priced at 1,000 ptas. Other boats offer longer trips, even to
the river mouth at Sanlucar de Barrameda, passing by the
Doñana National Park and wildlife sanctuary. Evening cruises are also featured, usually with music and flamenco.

Itálica

Scipio the African founded a Roman camp in 206 BC as a Rest and Recreation centre for his legions. In 45 B.C. the base was renamed Julia Romano by Julius Caesar, and it became one of Spain's most prosperous cities, with a 25,000-seater amphitheatre (third largest in the world), baths, houses paved with mosaics, and proper drains. Emperors Trajan and Hadrian were born here.

Only 7 miles north of central Seville, Itálica was used for many centuries as a handy quarry for building materials. The former richness of Itálica was well plundered, completing the demolition job done by the Vandals and the Arabs. Many Sevillian houses today are decorated with columns, statues and pieces of mosaic.

Some of the best finds are now safe in Seville's Archaeological Museum. Statues and reliefs from more recent excavations of a theatre are preserved in the on-site museum. Most of the original Itálica is still buried beneath the village houses of Santiponce.

In more recent times the Roman amphitheatre has been used for an International Dance Festival during July and August, with performances by top European ballet groups.

Córdoba

A visit to Córdoba – located 92 miles north of Seville – is the most rewarding whole-day excursion. On a do-it-yourself basis there are good bus and train connections. Otherwise you can sit back on a coach tour, travelling via Carmona and Ecija.

Already a large city when the Romans arrived in 206 BC, Córdoba's attraction dates mainly from the Moorish occupation which lasted from 572 to 1236 AD. That included periods of high civilization, when Córdoba ranked as the most splendid city of Europe, rivalling Baghdad and Byzantium as a dazzling centre of learning.

The greatest monument from that period is now the Cathedral, converted from one of Islam's finest mosques, the world's largest outside Mecca. Begun in 785 AD, the building was extended by successive rulers.

The cedar-wood ceiling is supported by a forest of 850 Roman and Visigoth columns of marble and granite, decorated with onyx and jasper. Horseshoe arches are striped red and white. Christian slaves made the lamps from recycled church bells.

Close by is the Judería, which has all the charm of Seville's Santa Cruz but less commercialized. Along the narrow, cobbled lanes you get numerous glimpses through wrought-iron grilles of tiled patios, balconies, and flowers everywhere. A synagogue dated 1316 still survives from the Jewish expulsion of 1492.

4.8 Sunday in Seville

Church Services

Sample a service at the Cathedral, and listen to the organ
and choir. Times of Sunday Mass at the High Altar – 10, 12
and 13 hrs; in the Royal Chapel – 8.30, 11, 17 & 18 hrs.

On weekdays, masses are held at 8.30, 9, 10, 12 & 17
hrs. Saturdays, at 13 and 19.30 hrs.

Museums & Galleries

Remember that most museums and galleries are open on
Sunday mornings, but closed on Mondays.

Street Markets

In true Spanish style, several street markets are held every
Sunday morning. There's a general flea market at Alameda
de Hércules and a pet market at Plaza de la Alfalfa.

The most central of these informal markets is at Plaza del
Cabildo – entrance just opposite west side of the Cathedral.
This gathering is devoted to stamps, coins and associated
collectibles; and also some paintings.

Other Sunday events

To enjoy a breath of open air, wander around María Luisa
Park and gravitate towards the Plaza de America. It's a
pleasant gathering point for young Sevillian families, with
children feeding the white doves while parents gossip in the
open-air cafe.

Bullfights

Even though football draws bigger crowds, all the ceremony
of the bullfight remains as a highlight of the middle-class
social calendar. Overall attendances are falling away, but
bull-fighting is still big business.

Bull-fighting is not regarded as a sport. It has almost a
religious idea of sacrifice, of man against the bull. There are
no variations to the ritual, rather like a formalized ballet
with blood and death to the main performers.

It's not everyone's choice for a Sunday afternoon, 5 p.m.
onwards between April and September, but matadors appear-
ing at Seville are usually the top stars.

4.9 Shopping in Seville

For the best cross-section of shopping in Seville, concentrate
on the area north of the Cathedral. Starting from Plaza Nueva, explore Calle de las Sierpes and its side and parallel
streets such as Velázquez Tetuán. Calle de las Sierpes itself

is a pleasant pedestrianised shopping street. Here you can find the full range of pottery for which Seville has a good reputation.

At 65 Sierpes is a tiled plaque in memory of Cervantes, who was imprisoned for non-payment of taxes in a gaol which occupied this spot. Here's where Cervantes called for writing paper, and began working on Don Quixote.

Top end of Sierpes, turn left into Plaza Duque de la Victoria – a pleasant palm-shaded square with central statue of Velázquez in full painting mode, brandishing a palette and brush. Along one side is the big chain department store, El Corte Inglés.

The square is filled with stalls which offer craft items such as fans, hippy-type jewelry and heavily-studded belts. You can buy charming readymade polka-dotted flamenco dresses for small girls.

Entire shops specialise in the sale of flamenco costume, both for women and children. The clientele is almost entirely local, getting ready for the next fiesta. Some of the costumes cost two or three hundred pounds. Look, for instance, in the 'Pardales' shop at Cuna 23 (parallel to Sierpes).

In the Santa Cruz district, souvenir shops are stacked high with mass-produced leather goods, mantillas, embroidery and castanets. Prices are substantially higher than elsewhere in town.

Unless something special catches your eye, make your purchases in some of the alternative locations mentioned above. Typically, colour film costs about one-third more than in non-tourist photo stores.

If you want to see craft-workers in action, visit El Postigo in Calle Arfe (west of the Cathedral) where a municipal building is used by members of the Andalusian Association for Craftsmanship.

Drugstores

For Drugstore requirements, several outlets are open all day till at least 1 a.m. – VIP'S till 3 a.m.

Cristina Multicentro, Almirante Lobo 5
Alameda Multicentro, Alameda de Hércules
Avenida Multicentro, Marqués de Paradas
VIP'S, República Argentina 23

Street Markets

A Thursday market of second-hand dealers is held around Calle de la Feria in the Macarena district.

Close by is Alameda de Hércules where a Sunday-morning flea market operates in the area overlooked by statues of Julius Ceasar and Hercules, perched on Roman columns. (See previous section for other Sunday markets.)

4.10 Eating Out in Seville

Andalusian specialities

The most evocative aromas of Seville are orange blossom and fried fish. Although the city lies well inland, many of the local restaurants specialize in excellent fish cuisine, with fresh supplies hauled up daily from Cadiz Bay.

Apart from the fish – mainly hake, swordfish, red mullet and whiting – here are some other specialities to give you a taste of Andalusia.

Pavias – a tapa of sliced cod, battered and deep fried
Gazpacho – the famous iced soup
Huevos a la sevillana – fried eggs on a foundation of onions, ham and tomatoes
Huevos a la flamenca – poached eggs with a sauce of oil, paprika, garlic and onion, topped with ham and varied vegetables
Cocido Andaluz – a very thick stew laced with chick-peas and everything that comes handy
Menudo de callos – a tripe dish with chick-peas and many added variables
Caldereta de cordero al estilo pastor – lamb stew, shepherd style
Rabo de toro – oxtail stew with hot peppers
Pestinos – honey fritters
Torrijas – a Holy Week special of white bread, dunked in wine or milk, dipped in batter, fried and sweetened with honey or sugar.
Yemas de San Leandro – prepared with egg yolk and sugar
Mostachónes – macaroons

Wines
Jerez (sherry); Montilla; Manzanilla; Malaga.

Restaurant Guide

Seville offers widest possible choice of restaurant from gourmet to fast hamburgers. They are well spread throughout the city, while anyone with a lesser appetite could easily absorb enough calories in the *tapas* bars.

The following suggestions are of restaurants that give added pleasure with their Andalusian decor or atmosphere. They are mostly in the two-fork range, which implies a meal at around £10-£15. To narrow the choice, they are roughly grouped according to district. Many restaurants offer a fixed-price menu for lunch, but then switch to more expensive à la carte only for dinner. Generally the restaurants around the popular Santa Cruz and Cathedral district are pricier than establishments across the river in Triana and Los Remedios.

Around the Cathedral and Santa Cruz

La Albahaca, Plaza de Santa Cruz 12   Tel: 422 0714
Located in a palace that has kept its atmosphere. Specialities:
fish dishes in distinctive Andalusian style.

Los Alcazares, Miguel de Mañara 10   Tel: 421 3103
A popular restaurant with a comfortable terrace, between the
Alcázar and the Lonja. Offers all the favourites of Andalusi-
an cuisine. Lunch from 12.30 hrs, dinner from 20.30 hrs.
Closed Sun.

El Giraldillo, Plaza Virgen de los Reyes 2 Tel: 421 4525
In the heart of the sightseeing action, with typical Sevillian
decor. Specialities: Andalusian paella, shrimps in garlic
sauce, shell fish casserole. Open 12-16 & 19.30-24 hrs.

La Hosteria del Laurel, Plaza de los Venerables 5
Colourful interior, or eat outdoors. Try their Spanish dry
sausages as tapas or as basis of a meal. Open 11-16 & 17-24
hrs. Closed Mon.   Tel: 522 0295

La Isla, Arfe 25   Tel: 421 2631
Round the back of Plaza del Cabildo, this restaurant features
a wide range of Spanish dishes, with the accent on fish.
Open 12-24 hrs. Closed Aug.

La Judería, Cano y Cueto 13   Tel: 441 2052
Located just outside the Santa Cruz district at Puerta de la
Carne, adjoining Murillo Gardens. Try their sucking lamb;
or the sea-bass. Closed Tue.

Modesto, Cano y Cueto 5   Tel: 441 6811
A neighbour to La Judería restaurant above, Modesto features seafood and fried fish. Modest prices. Closed Wed.

Mesón del Moro, Mesón del Moro 6 & 10
Italian cuisine pizza house, in a building of artistic and historic interest dating from around 1400. Reckon to pay at
least £12.   Tel: 421 4390

Mesón Don Raimundo, Argote de Molina 26
Housed in a 17th-century convent, very close to the Giralda.
Apart from the usual fish and seafood, they feature a range
of game dishes in Andalusian style. Open 12-17 & 19-24
hrs. Closed Sun night.   Tel: 422 3355

Egaña Oriza, San Fernando 41
Located near south end of Murillo Gardens. Basque and
international food. Closed Sun & Aug.   Tel: 422 7211

SEVILLE
North of the Cathedral

Casa Robles, Alvarez Quintero 58   Tel: 456 3272
Air conditioned, and very close to the Cathedral, north side.
Andalusian cuisine includes Ox Tail, Squids in their own
ink, Casserole of clams with ham and shrimp.

Mesón Castellano, Jovellanos 6   Tel: 421 4028
Go up Sierpes Street, and this restaurant is right next to San
José chapel on calle Jovellanos. They specialise in Castilian
cuisine, based particularly on grilled meat, with moderate
prices. Open 7-22 hrs.

San Marco, Cuna 6   Tel: 421 2440
Calle Cuna runs parallel to Sierpes, and the restaurant is at
the top end near Martin Villa. International and Italian cuisine includes Pheasant Ravioli, Toothed Bream, or Goose.
Open 13.15-16.00 & 20.15-24.00 hrs. Closed Sun and Aug.

María Luisa Park area

Luna Parque, Avenida María Luisa 1   Tel: 423 0006
Close to Lope de Vega theatre, with a summer terrace. On
Fridays and Saturdays, dinner with flamenco from 22 hrs till
early morning. Open 13-16 hrs & from 20 hrs onwards.

Julia "Los Monos", Avenida Molini 1   Tel: 461 3599
Next to María Luisa Park, near the Archaeological Museum.
Fish and seafood dominate the menu, including seafood
soups and casseroles, and Toothed Bream in Cognac Sauce.

Near the River

Bodegón Torre del Oro, c. Santander 15   Tel: 422 0880
Very close to Golden Tower. Specialities include Paella,
Garlic Chicken, Cheese Tart. Open: 19 hrs to 1.00 a.m.

Across the River – Triana and Los Remedios

El Puerto, calle Betis s/n   Tel: 427 1725
Open-air terraces, or a dining room with panoramic river
views. Offers a full range of fish. Closed Mon, and all Jan.

Asador Ox's, calle Betis 61   Tel: 427 9585
Traditional Basque cuisine with fish and roast meat. Closed
Sun night & Aug.

Bodegón El Riojano, Virgen de las Montanas 12
Specialities: Crawfish salad; Squid stuffed peppers; Partridge
with mushrooms. Open 13-16 & 21-01 hrs.   Tel: 445 0682

Rincón de Curro, Virgen de Luján 45   Tel: 445 0238
Takes pride in its red meat and great wine cellar. Or try
their mushroom and shrimp casserole, or Bass in Cleopatra
style.
Open 13-16 & 21-24 hrs. Closed Sun night and in August.

Rio Grande, calle Betis 70   Tel: 427 3956
Terraces offer wide views directly across the river to Torre
del Oro. Specialities: Hake with clams and baby eels; Ox
Tail; Home-style rice with clams and shrimp.
Open 13-17 & 20-24 hrs.

4.11 Nightlife

Seville has always had a great reputation for music, song
and dance from classics to the ever-popular flamenco.

The year's top annual event is the April Fair, celebrated
for six days and feverish nights with precise dates settled
each year by the City Council. Daytime horse parades are
followed by all the traditional night-time revelry, with colour
and costume everywhere. Be prepared for a mammoth jump
in hotel prices during this period.

Flamenco shows

Something of the traditional song and dance atmosphere is
conveyed by the city's flamenco shows. These night-spots
resound year-round to the clatter of castanets and the fantastic heel-drumming vitality of Spanish dance. Here are some
of the leading establishments.

El Patio Sevillano, Paseo Cristóbal Colón 11
Located on the river front, close to the bullring, this is rated
as the top show for flamenco and other regional dances,
some performed to taped music.

There are several shows nightly, sometimes simultaneous
in two small halls. Superb costumes, singing, dancing and
guitar-playing.   Tel: 421 4120

Buque El Patio   Tel: 421 1396
Has some linkage with El Patio Sevillano, using a flamenco
group for a 90-minute river-cruise performance. Embarcation
is at the Golden Tower Pier – Torre del Oro.

Los Gallos, Plaza de Santa Cruz 11   Tel: 421 6981
A smaller group, but in a superbly picturesque location in
the heart of Barrio Santa Cruz. It's a good quality show of
pure flamenco singing and dancing, but with smaller numbers of audience.

There are two shows a night, at 21 and 23.30 hrs.

SEVILLE

El Arenal, Calle Rodó 7   Tel: 421 6492
Open from 10 p.m. till 1.30 a.m. An authentic and colourful
show in a typical 17th-century Andalusian building with
appropriate decor. This *tablao* has capacity for 200 audience.

At last, an Opera House

Seville has been the setting for seven of the world's great
operas: "Don Giovanni", "Marriage of Figaro", "Barber of
Seville", "La Forza del Destino", "Fidelio", "La Favorita"
and the ever-popular image-creating "Carmen".

When the master plan for Expo '92 was first drafted, the
Cultural Activities Division proposed the inauguration of a
regular opera season devoted to the principal operas with
stories based on Seville. Curiously, though, the city had
lacked a purpose-built opera house.

That omission has been rectified with opening of the
Maestranza Theatre, devoted to opera and orchestral concerts. The theatre is located close to the Maestranza Bullring
and the Torre del Oro in central Seville.

Concerts and theatre performances are also given in the
Lope de Vega Theatre.

Finally there is a prestigious International Dance Festival
held every July and August in the Roman amphitheatre at
Itálica, just outside Seville.

Bars

Devote at least one evening to a *tasca*-crawl, stopping at a
selection of friendly little bars for a drink and some *tapas*.
In several areas, bars and characteristic restaurants are tight-
ly clustered. A prime location, for instance, is along the
narrow street called Mateos Gago, leading from the Giralda
and the Bishop's Palace.

Here, and in the side-streets that branch off, are numerous bars which are relatively small in relation to the number
of customers, especially on Friday and Saturday nights when
everyone spills out onto the highway and totally blocks the
traffic. The street scene itself becomes total theatre. There is
laughter and gossip everywhere.

Many establishments are centuries old. According to a
sign on a restaurant called Las Escobas: "This famous tavern
-in existence since 1386 - has been visited by men of science and letters, including Cervantes, Lope de Vega, Lord
Byron, Dumas, Becquer."

Turn right along Moro Street and you're into the much
quieter Santa Cruz quarter, which offers its own night-time
magic. Wrought-iron street lanterns make evocative patterns
against the grillework of windows and balconies. Little is
changed from long ago, apart from 20th-century conversion
to electric bulbs. Any moment you expect someone to start
singing bits from *The Barber of Seville*.

After nightfall, too, it's worth returning to admire the floodlit Giralda and Cathedral, standing clear and sharply against the sky. The lighting brings out the details even better than by day, showing up more strongly the pattern of the brickwork, the bells and the Giralda weathervane itself.

Another lively location is across the river to the Triana district. Bars, discos and restaurants are grouped thickly along the riverside between the bridges of San Telmo and Isabel II.

4.12 At your service in Seville

Banks & Exchange Bureaux
There are plenty of banks that operate weekdays till 14 hrs. Otherwise the main hotels can oblige, normally at less favourable rates.

Post Office & Telephone
Main Office: Avda. de la Constitución 32

Emergency telephone numbers
Police 091
Fire Brigade 442 0080

Other phone numbers and addresses
National Police: Plaza de la Gavidia   Tel: 422 8840
Local Police: Avda. de las Delicias   Tel: 461 5450

Lost Property
Calle Almansa Tel: 421 5694

Medical
Emergency Clinic, Jesús del Gran Poder 43 Tel: 438 2461
First Aid service – Casa de Socorro   Tel: 441 1712
Cruz Roja (Red Cross)   Tel: 435 0135
University Hospital, Avda. Dr. Fedriani   Tel: 437 8400
General Hospital, Avda. Manuel Siurot   Tel: 461 0000

Consulates
British: Plaza Nueva 8   Tel: 422 8875
American: Pabellon EE.UU, Paseo de las Delicias 7
                                               Tel: 423 1885
Canadian: Avda. de la Constitución 30   Tel: 422 9413

Tourist Information
In the main hall at San Pablo airport   Tel: 451 0677
at Avda. de la Constitución 21   Tel: 422 1404
and at Paseo de las Delicias 9   Tel: 423 4465

Chapter Five

Granada

5.1 Last outpost of the Moors

Let's go back five centuries. The year 1492 was the most dramatic in the history both of Granada and all Spain. It started brilliantly, on January 2nd, which is still observed as 'The Day of the Conquest'. On that day, 780 years of Muslim occupation ended with the surrender of Granada to the Christian monarchs.

Ferdinand and Isabella, united by marriage, were respectively King of Aragon and Queen of Castile – the two most powerful kingdoms of Iberia. Part of their prize was the 14th-century Alhambra – the Moorish 'Red Castle' which must rank among the world's most exquisite palaces.

The Muslim Sultans had been living in Granada almost 250 years longer than in Seville. Even though their territories were shrinking throughout that period, the Moorish rulers enjoyed great prosperity in a city that was a major medieval centre of art and learning. The population was then almost double that of today.

The Catholic monarchs adopted Granada as their capital. And there, after years of lobbying by Columbus, the contract was signed on April 17, 1492 to sponsor the navigator's historic voyage of discovery. It was a decision that brought immense wealth to Spain, to transform the following century into a Golden Age.

After the surrender of Granada, most of the wealthier Muslim citizens migrated back to Morocco, and immigrants from Castile took over their houses and lands. The remaining Muslims were squeezed into the Albaicín area at the foot of the Sacromonte. *See map, fig. 7.*

Under pressure from the Inquisition, these Muslims were given the choice in 1502 of expulsion or conversion to Christianity. Mosques became churches, and most of the Moorish baths were demolished.

Granada today is a city of 260,000 people, capital of Granada province, sandwiched between Cordoba province,

Malaga and Almeria, with a stretch of Mediterranean coast due south. Southeast of the city are the 3,400-metre peaks of the Sierra Nevada, highest in Europe outside the Alps. West lies La Vega – the plain of Granada – a richly fertile area watered by the River Genil.

In its unique setting on one of the spurs of the Sierra Nevada, Granada is a splendid jewel among the highlight cities of Andalusia. The whole atmosphere is bewitching.

In the Albaicín district – the original centre of the royal Arab court until the Alhambra was built – there are still many reminders of an Arab city. Amid the maze of narrow streets, pack-mules remain as a viable means of goods transport.

Close by are the remaining gipsy caves of Sacromonte, where sultry-looking girls with carnations in their jet hair dance flamenco every evening. It's commercialised, but very exciting.

Unifying all these impressions is the Royal Chapel where Ferdinand and Isabella are buried in magnificence: a reminder of the Catholic monarchs who changed the course of Spanish history five centuries ago.

To set the mood for a visit to Granada, dip into Washington Irving's 19th-century romantic *Tales of the Alhambra*.

5.2 Get your bearings

Start with the Gran Vía de Colón – Columbus High Street. That's the north-south axis which neatly splits Granada into two halves. At the south end of Gran Vía is the Cathedral and the Royal Chapel where Ferdinand and Isabella are buried. *See map, fig. 5.*

The T-junction street close by, marking the end of Gran Vía, is appropriately named Calle de los Reyes Católicos – Street of the Catholic Kings – running east-west.

Close by is Plaza Nueva, centre of commercial and tourist life, well supplied with hotels and restaurants. From that area, Cuesta de Gomérez climbs up to the Alhambra through Puerta de las Granadas. *See map, figs. 1 & 2.*

In the other direction, westwards, lies Plaza del Carmen with the Town Hall, and Puerta Real for the main Post Office. But most of Granada's sightseeing interest lies east of Gran Vía, within walking distance if you're energetic. Otherwise take a short taxi-ride: to the Alhambra, or the maze-like medieval streets of the Albaicín, or – furthest away – to the Sacromonte.

From downtown, bus no. 7 goes to the hill top of Albaicín, to Calle de Pagés, for a walk which should include the church of San Nicolás. From the terrace, a magnificent panoramic view takes in the Alhambra and the background snow-clad peaks of the Sierra Nevada.

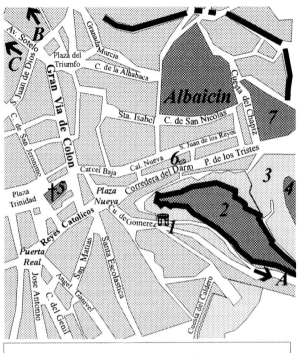

1 - Puerto de las Granadas - Gateway
2 - Alhambra
3 - Generalife Gardens
4 - Generalife Summer Palace
5 - Cathedral and Chapel Royal
6 - Moorish Baths
7 - Sacromonte Hill

➤ - Fortress walls

➔ A - towards Generalife entrance
   B - to Madrid 432 kms
   C - to Malaga 126 kms; Cordoba 172 kms

N

0 metres 400

GRANADA

5.3 Seeing basic Granada

The Alhambra   Tel: 22 7527

No other monument can bear better witness to the glory of
Spain's Moorish heritage. The Alhambra in Granada was
built in pure Arabian style, in contrast to the Alcázar of
Seville, which was a Mudejar mixture of Moorish and Christian architecture.

As the last Muslim stronghold in Iberia, Granada was
ruled by the Nasrid dynasty from the year 1237. At first
they lived in a fortress on the Albaicín hill, where defensive
walls still remain. But then they moved across to the neighbouring hill, and began building the Alhambra, which matured into a pleasure palace and a military and administrative
centre, totally ringed by walls and towers.

To explore the complex, allocate best part of a whole
day. Summer timings are Mon-Sat 9-20; Sun 9-18 hrs; winter closing at 17.45. Tickets are in three parts, giving admission to the Alcazabar, palaces and Generalife Gardens. To
avoid overcrowding, entrance to the palaces is spread on a
timed basis, within a half hour marked on the ticket. You
can explore the palace for as long as you like. But if you
miss the set entrance time, you cannot enter later. Separate
tickets are needed for the two museums – Fine Arts and
Hispano-Muslim Art – that occupy the Palace of Carlos V.

From the city centre, save your legs and take a taxi to
the ticket entrance; or catch bus no. 2 from Plaza Nueva.
Otherwise, on foot from Plaza Nueva, follow Cuesta de
Gomérez which climbs to the Alhambra through a 16th-century Renaissance gateway called Puerta de las Granadas.

Two woodland paths lead either to the Towers of Bermejas (built 1240 to replace a previous fortification), or to the
main entrance named Puerta de la Justicía.

The Gateway of Justice was built 1348: a massive square
tower with 50-ft sides, 66 ft high. The horseshoe-shaped
arch features two Islamic symbols: an outstretched hand and
a key. According to legend, the magic of the Alhambra will
be ended when the hand reaches down for the key.

The Alcazaba Fortress

This was Granada's original citadel, with foundations that go
back to Roman times. Located at the tip of the wooded
hillside, the Alcazaba offers a dominating view over the
town and Sacromonte, and of the snow-capped Sierra Nevada
mountain range.

The fortress was laid out in the classic style of Moorish
defence systems, with massive square towers overlooked by
the 13th-century Watch Tower – Torre de la Vela. Its large
bell was added in the 18th century.

GRANADA

The Alcázar Royal Palace – Casa Real

Here's one of the greatest sightseeing highlights of Spain: a perfect 14th-century Arabian-night palace, with rich history at every step through tiled courts, where cool water splashes from bronze fountains, and Moorish archways catch the hilltop breezes. Let's follow the recommended route:

Normal start of the Palace tour is through the **Mexuar** – the original council chamber which was later converted into a chapel, with an **Oratory** extension which offers a panorama of the Albaicín quarter.

Admire the panels of stucco and tiles of the **Mexuar Court**, and enter the **Court of the Myrtle Trees** – Patio de los Arrayanes – with a fish pond running down the centre. The north end is dominated by the severe military architecture of the Comares Tower, in contrast to the light-hearted fantasy of so much of the palace interior.

Hall of the Ambassadors

Approached through an antechamber called Sala de la Barca, the Throne Room or Hall of the Ambassadors was the audience chamber of the Sultans, who sat facing the entrance. With a cedar-wood ceiling, there are decorative inscriptions from the Koran or words of praise for King Yusuf 1 who built the Comares Palace during his reign 1333-1354.

Court of the Lions – Patio de los Leones

This delightful courtyard takes its name from the central fountain supported by a dozen barrel-chested lions. They guarded the State Apartments, including the harem, which led off from the light-hearted arcades supported by slim columns.

At the far end is the King's Chamber, where the ceilings of three alcoves are decorated with paintings on leather, portraying the Sultans and hunting scenes. This non-Islamic art was presumably the work of Castilian artists.

On the right-hand side of the Lion Court is the Hall of the Abencerrajes – named after numerous members of the Abencerraje family who were invited to a banquet, and who then lost their heads through suspicion that their chief had flirted or worse with the king's favourite wife. According to legend, the rust marks on the central fountain are really bloodstains. The lavish vaulting of the domed ceiling represents heaven.

On the opposite side of the Lion Patio is the Hall of the Two Sisters, represented by two slabs of white marble. This richly decorated Court with honeycomb ceiling was the main living room of the Sultan's favourite and other official wives. That leads into the Ajimeces Gallery and thence to the inner sanctum of the Mirador de Daraxa – Eyes of the Sultana – richly decorated with arabesques and a panelled ceiling.

Adjoining this inner harem area is the Daraxa Garden, tranquil with orange and cypress trees. A gallery leads in turn to the 17th-century Window Grille Court and down steps to the basement Royal Baths. Romantic writers from Washington Irving onwards have described a sumptuous and erotic lifestyle where the resident harem would bathe and relax, while blind singers and musicians supplied background entertainment. The Sultan would toss an apple to whichever lady he fancied for an hour or two.

Partal Gardens and the Towers

East of the main palace buildings are the Partal Gardens, with terraced pools, palm trees, water-lilies and roses galore. Here you can start a circuit of the perimeter walls and towers. From the Torre de las Damas (Ladies' Tower) there are superb views across to the Sacromonte hill and down to the River Darro below.

If you're feeling thirsty after all that, it's very pleasant to pause at the luxury-grade *Parador San Francisco* which originally was the Convent of Saint Francis. Queen Isabella was buried here until the Royal Chapel downtown was ready for her.

Carlos V Palace

In contrast to the Moorish architectural style of the original Alhambra, nothing could be further removed than the grey marble Renaissance palace begun during the reign of Emperor Charles V in the first half of the 16th century.

The design was by master architect Pedro Machuca, a former pupil of Michelangelo and of Raphael. The idea was to finance the building from taxes on citizens of Moorish origin. The project fell through when the queen became nervous after an earthquake, and the *Moriscos* rose in revolt in 1568. Work stopped for a few hundred years. The building was finally completed after the Spanish Civil War, and now houses two museums: Fine Art, and Hispano-Muslim Art (see next section).

The Generalife

Here was the Islamic dream of paradise – cool and green shaded gardens, with fountains and pools and running water. Laid out by the 14th-century Sultans, this summer retreat was extended and remodelled by the Catholic Monarchs. But the basic concept of the Generalife was retained with terraced water gardens and a lush growth of orange and cypress trees, oleanders, roses and water lilies. *See map, fig. 3.*

The buildings and pavilions of the summer palace *(fig. 4)* itself were relatively modest, but with superb views from several terraces. Certainly the Generalife must rate as the finest gardens of Spain, a sanctuary from the midday sun.

GRANADA

The Cathedral

Originally the site of the principal mosque, a gothic style Cathedral was planned soon after the re-conquest. Work began in 1523, to follow a similar architectural plan to that of Toledo Cathedral. *See map, fig. 5.*

Building was finally completed in 1704, after numerous changes of architect and building styles.

The Cathedral is open for sightseeing: in summer, Mon-Sat 10-10.30 and 16-19 hrs; Sun 16-19 hrs. In winter, 10.30-13.30 and 15.30-18.30 hrs. Tel: 22 2959

Royal Chapel

The monumental **Capilla Real** was built in richly ornamental gothic style between 1506-1517 as a somewhat ostentatious mausoleum for Ferdinand and Isabella. Queen Isabella's private collection of 15th-century Flemish, Spanish and Italian paintings is hung in the sacristy, and shouldn't be missed – especially rich in Memling.

Also on show is Isabella's golden crown and sceptre; and Ferdinand's sword.

The Chapel keeps the same visitor hours as the Cathedral, except on Sunday 11-13 hrs. Tel: 22 9239

5.4 Other sights in Granada

Museums and Galleries

National Museum of Hispano-Muslim Art, Alhambra
Ground floor of the Palace of Charles V, adjoining the Court of the Myrtle Trees. Tel: 226279
A collection from all periods of Muslim Spain, but richest in artefacts of the Nasrid era of Granada. A dozen halls display glazed tiles and stucco work, marble and wooden items, marquetry and furniture.

The Moorish art collection is regarded as the finest in Spain. The prize exhibit is the blue 14th-century 'Alhambra vase' which originally stood in the Hall of the Two Sisters.
Open: 9-14.30 hrs. Closed: Sun and Mon.

Museum of Fine Art, Alhambra Tel: 22 4843
Upstairs in the Palace of Charles V
Specialized in 17th-century paintings of the Granada school. The principal names are Alonso Cano who was also an architect, responsible for the Cathedral facade; Pedro Bocanegro, whose work shows Flemish and Italian influences; and Friar Sanchez Cotan, a Carthusian monk who was an innovator of Tenebrism – using large areas of darkness pierced by shafts of light.
Open: 10-14 hrs. Closed: Sun and Mon.

House and Museum of Lorca, Fuentevaqueros

A ten-mile bus ride departing from Avenida de Andaluces –
by the railway station – to the village of Fuentevaqueros.
The family home where Federico Garcia Lorca was born in
1899, in the village which inspired much of his poetry.
However, his most famous poem *Romancero Gitano* (Gipsy
Ballads) used the traditional ballad form and rhythms of the
Andalusian gipsies.

Shot by Franco's men in 1936, Lorca is still among the
best-known literary figures of 20th-century Spain. The house
is open to the public, and has become a place of pilgrimage
for admirers of his work.

Open: 10-13 & 17-19 hrs, but check times first, before
travelling! Closed: Mon.

Huerte de San Vicente, Garcia Lorca House Tel: 258466

Another Lorca house-museum containing furniture and personal belongings of the poet who used it as a summer retreat
from 1925 onwards. Devotees can obtain a pass from the
cultural department of Granada Town Hall. The house is
located behind the Neptune Gardens, and has a good view of
the Alhambra.

Open: Tue-Sun 10-13 & 17-20 hrs in summer; or 10-13 &
16-19 in winter.

House and Museum of Manuel de Falla   Tel: 229421

Located next to Hotel Alhambra, Callejon de Falla

A simple house where much of Manuel de Falla's music was
composed, so evocative of southern Spain.

Born 1876 in Cádiz, Falla lived from 1914 onwards
mainly in Granada, which inspired such works as 'Nights in
the Gardens of Spain', and 'El Amor Brujo' ('Love the
Magician') based on legends of the local gipsies.

A close friend of Lorca, Falla left Spain and died 1946 in
Argentina. Next door is the Manuel de Falla Auditorium,
where an International Music and Dance Festival is held
every year.

Open: Tue-Sat 10-15 hrs. Entrance: 250 ptas.

Gomez Moreno Museum   Tel: 227497

Next to Alhambra Palace Hotel on Calle Nino del Royo

A personalized collection of books, ceramics, paintings and
sculptures, formed by Gomez Moreno (1834-1918) who
made Granada his life's study.

Open: Tue-Sat 10-13.30 hrs. Entrance: free.

San Jerónimo Monastery   Tel: 27 9337

St Jerome's 16th-century monastery church is the oldest and
largest of Granada's churches, founded in 1520, one year
before the Cathedral. Open: 10.00-13.30 & 16-19 hrs.

GRANADA

La Cartuja Monastery

A wildly exuberant Carthusian monastery, lavishly decorated with Baroque stucco, with elaborate and costly use of marble, silver and gold.

Open: 10-13 & 16-20 hrs. Sun 10-12 hrs.   Tel: 16 1932

El Bañuelo – Moorish Baths

Along the narrow Carrera del Darro which runs beside the little River Darro are the Arab Baths at no. 31 on the corner of Calle Baruelo. *See map, fig. 6.* The well preserved baths were founded in 11th century.

Open: Tue-Sat 10-14 hrs.   Tel: 22 2339

Archaeological Museum

At 43 Carrera del Darro (very close to the Moorish Baths) is a Renaissance mansion named **Casa de Castril**, which features a number of finds from early cave-dwellers in Granada Province. The Moorish collection comprises some fine works of art.

Open: Tue-Sun 10-14 hrs.   Tel: 22 5640

5.5 Take a trip

During winter it's possible to combine Granada with a taste of skiing on the most southerly slopes in Europe. Only 20 miles from Granada is the purpose-built ski resort of Sierra Nevada – also known as Solynieve, which means Sun'n'-Snow. The Veleta peak, 3,392 metres, is among the highest in Spain.

The slopes above 2,100 metres offer good potential for beginners and intermediate level skiers, with somewhat fewer runs for the expert. As the host resort for the 1995 Alpine World Championships, big sums were spent on ensuring international standards.

For a day trip, there are two coaches daily in summer, four in winter. Check timings from the operator: Viajes Bonal, Tel: 27 3100.

5.6 Shopping

Local craft products can still convey a feeling of North Africa, even though the Moorish rulers departed five centuries ago. The basic skills remained and flourished, following traditions handed down through generations of *moriscos* – the Muslims who converted to Christianity.

There's a parallel with the Mudéjar style of architecture, where Arabic craftsmanship was adapted to suit Catholic clients.

Especially look for Fajalauza glazed pottery, with green and blue designs on a white base. Several workshops are grouped in the Albaicín district. In more recent times, young potters have moved into Granada province, and are producing unglazed earthenware which revive traditional styles.

Likewise Moorish-type craftmanship in embossed leather still finds a ready market. The metal trades – especially copperware, and wrought iron products such as lanterns – continue to follow traditional designs.

There's every variation on marquetry, using inlaid wood and mother-of-pearl to garnish jewelry boxes and miscellaneous trivia. Canny old gipsy ladies with multilingual gift of the gab besiege visitors to buy lace items, embroidery and mantillas.

If you don't have time to seek out the direct-sell workshops, here are some shopping locations to investigate:

La Alcaiceria – next to the Cathedral, reconstructed in Moorish style, was a silk bazaar in medieval times.

Corral del Carbón – just off calle Reyes Católicos, was originally a 13th-century caravanserai for travelling Arab merchants. The building had several changes of use over the centuries, including use of the interior courtyard as a theatre, but now is a crafts market endorsed by the State-operated Artespaña.

Other craft stores are clustered in the area of **Plaza Nueva** and **Cuesta de Gomérez** – the approach route to the Alhambra.

5.7 Eating Out in Granada

Just like in Seville, Granada offers all the Andalusian food specialities, with fried fish in abundance. A local dish worth trying is the gipsy-style **tortilla Sacromonte**, a ham and shrimp omlette with green vegetables – though the full meaty version can include poached brains and lamb's testicles, which you're unlikely to get in restaurants that cater for foreign visitors.

Another great speciality is **habas con jamón** – broad beans with Trevelez cured ham. You can also find the local broad beans in a casserole called **cazuela de habas**, and in numerous thick stews with varied meat ingredients.

Long occupation by the sweet-toothed Moors has left a tradition of very sweet confectionery.

If you want to explore the *tapas* circuit, try around Plaza de la Trinidad (a few blocks due west of the Cathedral, along Calle Capuchinas); or on Campo del Príncipe (half a mile south-east of Plaza Nueva); or in the area around Plaza Gran Capitán.

Numerous restaurants are located between Plaza Nueva and the Cathedral.

5.8 Nightlife

Flamenco shows

Just like Seville, Granada lays claim to the most 'genuine' of flamenco. Granada's traditional centre of this entertainment is among the gipsy cave-dwellers of Sacromonte. For over 400 years gipsies were settled in a rabbit-warren of caves burrowed into the chalky hillside.

There they earned a living from the traditional gipsy trades: dealing in horses and donkeys, making pots and pans, telling fortunes, begging and – most famous of all – in entertaining with song and dance to the sound of guitars and castanets.

After big floods in 1962, the gipsies were rehoused in high-rise apartments elsewhere. Some cave dwellings today are used by university students for weekend discos. But a few gipsy caves still operate in traditional style on the Sacromonte hillside. For some time the gipsies gave themselves a poor reputation, through their hard-sell tactics in wheedling every last peseta for a poor performance.

But generally they now give better value for money. With an electrifying rattle of castanets and clash of tambourines, the gipsies perform with a passion that makes other countries' folk-dancing seem lifeless.

A local operator features a night tour, based on a stroll through the Albaicín, a panoramic view of the floodlit Alhambra seen from the San Nicolás Mirador, followed by a gipsy flamenco show with drink included and safe return to your hotel by coach around midnight.

For details phone 224525 or 222492.

The Alhambra by moonlight

Occasionally night-time music recitals are held in the Alhambra. A concert can be pure magic when heard in such a perfect setting.

During the main season, the Alhambra can also be visited between 22 hrs and midnight on guided tours, usually Tuesday, Thursday and Saturday nights.

The International Festival of Music and Dance

This prestigious event is held annually from mid-June to mid-July, and gives opportunities to enjoy music in the Alhambra. Some ballet and dance programmes are given in the Generalife gardens, and other performances in the Carlos V Palace. Soloists give recitals in the Court of the Myrtles. Finally the Manuel de Falla Auditorium is rated among the finest in Europe, with superb acoustics.

Tickets are available from Comisaría del Festival, Corral del Carbón, Calle Liberos 2. Tel: 222111.

5.9 At your service in Granada

Main Post Office & Telephone
Puerta Real, at western end of Calle de los Reyes Católicos.
Open Mon-Fri 9-14 hrs

Emergency telephone number
Police 091

English newspapers
Check the kiosks on Plaza Nueva, by the Cathedral and
opposite the Tourist Information Office on Plaza Mariana
Pineda.

Consulates
Canada – Pl. Malagueta 3   Tel: 22 3346
Ireland – c. General Mola, Fuengirola near Malaga
                                                Tel: 47 5108
UK – calle Duquesa de Parcent 3   Tel: 21 7541
USA – Edif. El Ancla Room 502, c. Ramon y Cajal, Fuen-
girola near Malaga   Tel: 47 4891

Tourist Information
Provincial Tourist Office, Plaza Mariana Pineda 10. Open
Mon-Fri 9.30-19.00 hrs; Sat 10-14 hrs.   Tel: 22 6688

Tourist Office (Andalusia), Corral del Carbón, calle Liberos
2 (just off the Calle Reyes Católicos).
Open Mon-Sat 9-19 hrs; Sun 10-14.   Tel: 22 5990

Chapter Six

Further information

6.1 Explore Spanish cuisine

All restaurants are classifed by forks: a five-fork establishment is luxury grade; down to one-fork. No forks, use your fingers. Cafeterias are rated from one to three cups. These grades are a good indicator of the price levels to expect. A menu turistico is offered by all cafeterias and one- to three-fork restaurants, and should cost no more than 80% of the total price of the separate items. The basic menu is always displayed by the entrance, so you can easily shop around.

Spanish meal timings are very non-EEC. Restaurants are open to serve midday meal from 1 p.m. to 4 p.m.; dinner from 8 p.m. till midnight. But, despite having a very light continental breakfast of rolls or doughnuts, many Spaniards do not think of lunch till 2 p.m., and the evening meal from 10 p.m.

The idea – quite sensible in Spain's summer climate – is to take a break in the hottest part of the afternoon, to resurface fresh for another few hours' work followed by social life.

With air conditioning, the need for a full siesta is declining. But the mealtime pattern remains unchanged. Hence the great tapas institution. Like very prolonged starters or appetizers, or blotting paper, tapas can save you from dropping with hunger while you drink wine with your friends either before lunch or dinner.

Tapas are small snacks which encourage you to keep drinking in bars, instead of going off to a proper meal.

Many bars specialise in tapas. You can choose what you fancy, just by pointing. Dishes include prawns with garlic, marinated olives, potato salad, baby eels, kidney beans in vinegar sauce, pickled cauliflower, pig's trotters in garlic sauce, meat-balls, mushrooms in garlic, potato croquettes, you-name-it.

Many of the tapas can be heated. It's possible to spend more for a full range of tapas than for a regular dinner.

Restaurant meals

Spanish meals are hearty rather than nouvelle cuisine. Cooking is based on olive oil and heavy-handed use of garlic. The soups are often very filling: fish; broth with sausage, beans, etc. If your spoon goes missing, these sturdy soups can be eaten with a fork.

Quite apart from the regional specialities, you'll obviously be well exposed to all the rich potential of Spanish cuisine, regardless of which city you're visiting. Look out for these specialities:

Gazpacho – a refreshing cold soup of chopped-up raw cucumber, tomatoes, olive oil, peppers and garlic, with vinegar, oil and ice.

Cocido – a thick stew with basic chick peas, meat or bacon, potatoes and other vegetables. Almost a full meal in itself.

Bacalao (cod) – cooked in dozens of different styles, here's the favourite traditional fish which shares sea-food menus with hake (merluza) and sea bream (besugo).

Paella – ingredients can be highly varied: saffron rice, prawns, mussels, chicken, rabbit, sausage, peas, red peppers, almost anything that comes to hand.

Tortilla Española – potato omelette, often sold cold and stodgy.

Guide to menu items

Entremeses

Starters

Aceitunas	Olives
Anchoas	Anchovies
Caracoles	Snails
Chorizo	Spicy pork sausage, salami
Ensalada	Salad
Ensaladilla rusa	Russian salad
Entremeses variados	Mixed hors d'oeuvres
Esparragos	Asparagus
Gambas	Prawns
Jamón serrano	Smoked ham
Ostras	Oysters

Sopas

Soups

Sopa de ajo	Garlic soup
de cebolla	Onion soup
de gallina	Chicken soup
de mariscos	Shellfish soup
de pescado	Fish soup
de verduras	Vegetable soup
Gazpacho	Cold soup of tomatoes etc

INFORMATION

Pescados Fish

Spain is very rich in seafood, ranging from calamares to zarzuela (a comic opera of fish and shellfish laced with wine and brandy). Fast refrigerated transportation ensures that Madrid, Seville and Granada can be just as well served with fresh seafood as Barcelona.

Anguila	Eel
Atun	Bonito
Bacalao	Cod
Bullabesa	Catalan style of fish stew
Calamares en su tinta	Squid cooked in their own ink
Cangrejo	Crab
Centolla	Spider crab
Gambas a la plancha	Grilled prawns
Langosta	Lobster
Lenguado	Sole
Lubina	Sea-bass
Mejillones	Mussels
Merluza	Hake
Pez espada	Swordfish
Raya	Skate
Rodaballo	Turbot
Sardinas a la plancha	Grilled sardines
Zarzuela de mariscos	Seafood casserole

Carne Meat dishes

Although Spain is the land of brave bulls, it takes courage and tenacity to work through some of the beef. Lamb is a far better bet. Or why not venture on sucking-pig, or stewed kid? If you are prejudiced against veal – ternera – remember that the animal was more grown-up than most European veal: it's almost beef.

Albondigas	Rissoles
Butifarra	Catalan sausage
Cabrito asado	Roast sucking goat
Carne de venado	Venison
Carnero	Mutton
Cerdo	Pork
Chuleta	Chop
Cochinillo/toston	Sucking-pig
Conejo	Rabbit
Cordero asado	Roast lamb
Embutidos	Sausages
Fabada	Pork and bean stew
Guisado de ternera	Veal stew
Higado	Liver

Lengua	Tongue
Morcilla	Blood pudding
Pato	Duck
Pechuga	Breast of chicken
Pollo	Chicken
Pote gallego	Hotpot
Salchichas	Sausages
Ternera a la Jardinera	Beef and vegetable casserole
Vaca	Beef

Arroz   Rice dishes

Italy has its pasta; Spain goes for rice, which has been grown in large quantities in the Valencia region since its introduction by the Moors in the 8th century. Originally the Paella or Arroz dishes were part of poor man's cuisine, mostly saffron-coloured rice with a little meat or fish to flavour. Prosperity has changed the balance, and now the meat or seafood ingredients are the principal element. The word 'paella' is the name of the heavy iron two-handled pan in which the food is cooked, and served on the table.

Arroz catalana	Rice with pork, sausages and fish
Arroz marinera	Rice with seafood
Paella valenciana	Saffron rice with seafood and chicken

Legumbres   Vegetables

Spain is rich in vegetables and salads. Vegetables are often served as a starter, either cold or perhaps lightly fried with diced ham and tomato. It's usual to order a mixed salad with the main course. Stewed dishes are mostly based on the pulses such as lentils, dried beans and chick peas.

Ajo	Garlic
Alubias	French beans
Apio	Celery
Berenjena	Aubergine
Cebolla	Onions
Champiñón	Mushroom
Coles	Brussels sprouts
Esparragos	Asparagus
Espinacas	Spinach
Garbanzos	Chickpeas
Guisantes	Peas
Judías	Beans
Lechuga	Lettuce
Lentejas	Lentils

INFORMATION

Patata	Potato
Pepino	Cucumber
Pimiento	Pepper
Remolacha	Beetroot
Repollo	Cabbage
Zanahoria	Carrot

Huevos   Egg dishes

There are dozens of egg-cuisine variations – fried, poached, baked or in omelette (tortilla) style.

Tortilla francesa	Plain omelette
Huevos revueltos	Scrambled eggs
Huevos a la Turca	Poached eggs with tomato etc

Postres y Frutas   Desserts, fruits etc

Spanish pastries are mostly over-sweet, and many visitors prefer to enjoy the splendid range of fresh fruit. According to season there are oranges (naranjas), melons (sandía or melon), grapes (uvas), peaches (melocotones), dates (datiles), strawberries (fresas), apricots (albaricoques), figs (higos).

Cheese? The most popular is manchego, from La Mancha, which comes in a variety of shapes and flavours. For a blue cheese, try queso cabrales made from a mixture of goat, sheep and cows' milk.

The Wine List

The leading table wines of Spain come from Castile, especially La Rioja, and from the Central Spain area of La Mancha, with Valdepeñas among the most popular. In general, the Spaniards do not go overboard on years and vintages, though classic wines are labelled in strict compliance with EEC regulations.

Supermarkets and bars alike are stacked high with an enormous range of wines from every region of Spain. The Rioja wines are available throughout Spain, especially Siglo Saco (red), Vina Sol (dry white), San Valentín (sweet white), and Torres (rosé).

In general, the Rioja wines can rival Bordeaux or Burgundy on quality, but some of the cheaper Rioja Baja wines are pretty rough.

For an everyday regional wine, ask for vino corriente or vino comun.

Sangría is a popular drink – a mixture of red wine, orange and lemon juice, brandy, mineral water, slices of fruit and plenty of ice. It's very refreshing, but rather heavy to drink with a meal. Sangría is potent stuff. Watch it!

Sherry is the great aperitif. The dry fino and medium amontillado are drunk chilled, especially before meals with tapas. Manzanilla wines are very close to the finos. Sweet sherries – oloroso and dulce – are used as dessert wines.

Among the stronger drinks, Spain is well known for its range of brandies, mostly sweeter and heavier than cognac. Good medium-priced ones include Mango "103" and Carlos III. One of the best, comparable to a French cognac, is Carlos I.

A popular nightcap is Sol y Sombre, a mixture of brandy and anis.

Spain also produces several sweet or over-sweet liqueurs, many made under license. If you order an after-dinner Cointreau, a serving looks like half a tumbler.

The principal local beer is a light lager type, with good flavour. Leading brands are San Miguel, Cruzcampo and Aguila.

Non-alcoholic drinks

Most holidaymakers are nervous about drinking the local tap water flavoured with chlorine, though city water is perfectly safe. If you prefer caution with bottled mineral water, ask for agua mineral. For a simple bottle of sweet and fizzy lemonade, ask for Sprite. Otherwise, there's the usual choice of Pepsi, Fanta or Coke.

English-type tea with milk is best avoided, except in tea-shops that cater specially for the Brits. However, at buffet-style breakfasts you could experiment with the hotel-supplied tea bags, and see how it tastes.

Breakfast coffee in hotels is usually French style, or instant powdered. In a bar or restaurant, ask for *café solo* (without milk), *café cortado* (with a little milk), *café con leche* (white coffee), or *carajillo* (black coffee with a shot of brandy or rum).

The normal Spanish breakfast is very light: café con leche (half coffee, half milk) and a pastry. Breakfast in a bar is often based on *churros* – fritters cooked before your eyes in boiling oil. These often make a popular afternoon snack with very thick hot drinking-chocolate.

Drinks

Tea	té
Milk	leche
Orange juice	zumo de naranja
Wine	vino
Beer	cerveza
Mineral water	agua mineral
…fizzy	agua con gas
…still	agua sin gas
Cheers!	¡Salud!

INFORMATION

6.2 Travellers' Vocabulary

Don't worry if you cannot speak Spanish. In the main hotels, restaurants, bars and shops, service staff have at least a smattering of most West European languages. If not, there's always someone handy who can translate.

However, there's pleasure in being able to use and recognise even just a few words. Don't worry about the accents. Apart from ñ (pronounced as in onion), the accents merely indicate the syllable to stress. Otherwise they don't change the vowel sound.

There are regional variations. In pure Castilian, 'c' and 'z' emerge mostly as a 'th' sound; but in Andalusia they are more like variants of 's'. Again, don't let it bother you, unless you're studying for O-level.

If you're visiting Barcelona, another complication: the Catalans take pride in fostering their own language. Derived from Latin, Catalonian dates from the time when Barcelona was a thriving Roman city. In medieval times, Catalonia spread into what today is Provence in southern France.

Over the centuries the Catalan language was banned by the central government of Madrid. In more recent years, Catalan has thrived legally. It is the principal language of instruction in schools, though virtually everyone ends up bilingual.

Showing its independence of Castilian, Catalan is liberally sprinkled with x's, and the stress accents slope t'other way round. Most Barcelona menus are printed in both Catalan and Castilian; with luck, also in English.

For the beginner in Spanish, the following page gives a starter kit of a few words to show you're trying.

Greetings

Hello	hola
Goodbye	adiós
Good morning	buenos días
Good afternoon	buenas tardes
Good evening	buenas noches
How are you?	¿como esta usted?
Very well, thank you	muy bien, gracias

General

Yes	sí
No	no
Please	por favor
Thank you	gracias
Do you speak English?	¿habla usted inglés?
I don't understand	no comprendo
What time is it?	¿que hora es?

INFORMATION

Shopping

Bank	banco
Bookshop	librería
Currency exchange	cambio
Chemist	farmacia
Doctor	médico
Hairdresser	peluqueria
Newspaper kiosk	puesto de periódicos
Supermarket	supermercado
Tobacconist	estanco
Post office	correos
Stamps	sellos
Postcard	postal
How much is it?	¿cuánto es?

Signs

Abierto	open
Ascensor	lift/elevator
Caballeros	gents
Caliente	hot
Cerrado	shut
Empujar	push
Entrada	entrance
Frio	cold
Libre	vacant
Ocupado	occupied
Prohibido entrar	no entrance
Prohibido fumar	no smoking
Salida	exit
Salida de emergencia	emergency exit
Señoras	ladies
Tirar	pull

Numbers

0	cero

1-10 uno, dos, tres, cuatro, cinco, seis, siete, ocho, nueve, diez

11-19 once, doce, trece, catorce, quince, dieciséis, diecisiete, dieciocho, diecinueve

20-29 veinte, veintiuno, veintidós, veintetrés etc

30-39 treinta, treinta y uno, treinta y dos, etc

40, 50...-90 – cuaranta, cincuenta, sesenta, setenta, ochenta, noventa

100	cien/ciento
101	ciento uno
200	doscientos
500	quinientos
1000	mil
2000	dos mil
1,000,000	un millón

INFORMATION

Sightseeing

Where is ...?	¿Dónde está... ?
the beach	la playa
the bridge	el puente
the bus stop	la parada de autobús
the castle	el castillo
the church	la iglesia
the information office	la oficina de informationes
the museum	el museo
the port	el puerto
the square	la plaza
the station	la estación
the street	la calle

6.3 Who's Who in the Arts

Albéniz, Isaac – A child prodigy pianist, 1860-1909, he first performed in public at age 4. He studied at the Madrid Conservatoire, but skipped to USA as a 12-years-old stowaway to earn his living as a pianist. He returned to Europe, settled finally in Paris, but composed entirely in a style imspired by the music and dance rhythms of Spain, particularly of Andalusia.

Cervantes, Miguel – Author of *Don Quixote*, Cervantes was born 1547, died 1616, and was dogged with even more of life's misfortunes than the literary character he created. Cervantes lost his left hand in the Battle of Lepanto, and was imprisoned 5 years in Algiers. As a government servant he travelled extensively in Andalusia, and started his famous novel when gaoled in Seville for non-payment of taxes. A major monument to Cervantes, Don Quixote, Sancho Panza and Rosinante is located in Madrid's Plaza de España.

Dalí, Salvador – Surrealist painter, 1904-1989, studied in Madrid and was closely associated with Spanish modernists such as Lorca and Buñuel. Dalí created a bizarre world that was reflected in his own personal style of handlebar moustache, popping eyes and flowing capes. A museum at Figueres near Barcelona is dedicated to his work.

El Greco – 'The Greek' was born in Crete 1541, and first painted Byzantine-style ikons; then studied in Venice and Rome, before arriving 1577 in Toledo to undertake a set of religious paintings. The dramatic intensity of his style did not please the court, so El Greco remained in Toledo until his death in 1614. His legacy to Toledo is the number of his masterpieces which attract thousands of visitors on day trips from Madrid, where the Prado also has a rich collection.

INFORMATION

Falla, Manuel de – The most Spanish of composers, de Falla (1876-1946) studied piano in Madrid but spent much of his life in Granada. He drew themes from the local gypsies and from Andalusia folk music.

Gaudí, Antonio – Modernist architect, 1852-1926, who enlivened Barcelona with eccentric Art Nouveau buildings which are among the city's principal sightseeing attractions. His unfinished cathedral, La Sagrada Familia, is a landmark that still arouses great controversy.

Gonzalez, Julio – Abstract sculptor in welded iron, 1876-1942, Gonzalez first studied painting for six years in Barcelona before moving to Paris. As a Cubist painter, he was greatly influenced by his contemporary, Picasso. Later he switched to metalwork sculpture.

Goya, Francisco – A brilliant artist, 1746-1828, Goya settled in Madrid from 1774 and initially produced cartoons for the Royal Tapestry Factory. Appointed as court painter in 1786, his portraits were in constant demand even though the end result was often unflattering. The Prado has the world's finest collection of his work.

Granados, Enrique – Composer and pianist, 1867-1916, Granados studied in Barcelona, Madrid and Paris, and established his own academy of music in Barcelona from 1889. His piano suite *Goyescas* is based upon Goya's tapestries and paintings, while his *12 Spanish Dances* are equally evocative of the national idiom.

Herrera, Juan – An architect, 1530-1597, he was responsible for the Escorial, considered as one of Europe's finest Renaissance buildings. His austere, symetrical style can also be seen in the Alcázar of Toledo and in the Archive of the Indies building in Seville. The Herreriano style is reflected in the work of other 16th-century architects.

Lorca, García – Spain's greatest 20th-century poet and playwright, born 1898 in Granada where he was shot by a Franco firing squad in 1936. *Blood Wedding* is part of a trilogy regarded as his masterpiece.

Miró, Joan – A leading light in abstract and surrealist art, 1893-1983, Miró studied in Barcelona until he moved to Paris in 1919. Although in close contact with Picasso and the Cubists, he experimented with dream-inspired art which led him to joining the surrealist movement. Later he turned to ceramics, murals and tapestry design. The Miró Foundation in Barcelona displays the wide range of his art.

INFORMATION

Murillo, Bartolomé – A prolific baroque painter, 1617-1682, was born in Seville where he worked most of his life, with an interlude in Madrid to study Italian Renaissance works. Many buildings in Seville display his canvases, and there are more in the Prado.

Picasso, Pablo – The 20th century's most famous and influential artist, 1881-1973, Picasso first displayed his ability as a 14-years-old advanced student at the Barcelona Academy of Fine Arts. Hundreds of books have described every facet of his dazzling career. Barcelona's Picasso Museum is exceptionally rich in his earliest notebook sketches. Madrid's greatest prize is Picasso's awesome *Guernica*.

Vega, Lope de – A dazzling product of the Spanish Golden Age, he was born 1562 in Madrid, died 1635. He wrote around 800 plays, hundreds of poems, short stories and other works. Yet he still found time for numerous love affairs, service with the Spanish Armada, two marriages and entry into the priesthood.

Velázquez, Diego – Born in Seville 1599, died 1660, Velázquez was apprenticed at age 12 and attained master status at age 18. By age 24 he moved to Madrid and was appointed court painter to Philip IV, who remained his patron the rest of his life. Many of his superb portraits are in the Prado. He is regarded as the greatest of Spain's baroque artists.

Zurbarán, Francisco – Another baroque artist from Seville, 1598-1664, Zurbarán followed his contemporary Velázquez in his dramatic use of light and shadow contrasts (chiaroscuro) in religious paintings, with brilliant colours and fine detail. His style greatly influenced Murillo, who took over in popularity during his later years.

6.4 At your service in Spain

Changing Money
You can readily change money and travellers cheques at arrival airports, banks, exchange bureaux and larger hotels. You need to produce your passport. Commission rates vary and can be higher in hotels. Check first. Generally banks deduct a flat-rate minimum commission, making it uneconomic to change small sums of money.

Credit cards
All the principal cards are generally accepted in Spain, especially in centrally located shops, hotels and restaurants. You should have no problems with major plastic.

Eurocheques

Eurocheques are a safe and common method of payment. They can be obtained from your bank if ordered in advance. Eurocheques are readily accepted for currency exchange, and are widely used in shops, restaurants etc when presented with a valid Eurocheque card. Numerous cash dispensers are open for use by cardholders. Look out for the blue and red "ec' sticker.

Currency

Spanish currency is the Peseta, often abbreviated to Pts or ptas. For a quick guide to price levels, reckon something under 200 Pesetas to the pound, or 125 Pesetas to the dollar. Check the current exchange rate for more accurate calculations.

Coins are of 1, 5, 10, 25, 50, 100 and 200 Pesetas. Banknotes arc in denominations of 200, 500, 1000, 2000, 5000 and 10,000 Pts.

Tipping

If you're staying more than a few days, don't forget your waiters and chambermaids. Tipping is entirely optional, depending on how good and friendly the service has been. If in doubt, ask your Rep for guidance on how much.

In restaurants, a service charge is usually included, even if it's not shown separately. But satisfied customers still leave a further 5% or 10% – likewise for table service in bars. For hairdressers and taxi drivers about 10% is normal. On coach excursions, a tip is shared between the guide and driver.

Electricity

220-volt AC, using continental style 2-pin plugs. Pack an appropriate plug adaptor for any appliances you take. You can easily buy adaptors in supermarkets or electronic stores.

Spanish Time

Spain is on GMT plus one hour – the same time zone as most of Western Europe. Hence Britain is usually one hour behind, but also gets out of step through choosing different dates to switch between summer and winter times. So take care when adjusting your watch in late March and September/October!

North America: Eastern Standard Time is six hours behind Spain.

Phoning to Spain

City dialling codes from UK are: 00 – then 34-3 for Barcelona; 34-1 for Madrid; 34-54 for Seville; 34-58 for Granada. Dialling from USA or Canada: 011 – then codes as above.

INFORMATION

Phoning home

Calls made from your hotel room are hassle-free; but most hotels at least double the cost onto your bill. For an international call, the price can be a shock if you talk too long. To save money, try using a street or Post Office call-box.

To operate a pay phone, collect a stack of 25 and 100 peseta coins. Line them along the diagonal slope on the phone, before dialling. The first coin drops down when the connection is made, and more coins are eaten automatically as the seconds tick by. Keep the slot well fed, and you can remove any leftover coins when you hang up.

For international calls: dial 07 and wait for the tone to change; then dial country code (UK 44) + local area code minus the first 0; then the local number.

Seeing those 100-peseta coins disappear rapidly down the slot is a constant reminder to cut the cackle. Say anything important first, in case the call cuts off, or your coins run out, or the coin-box chokes because it cannot take any more money. Encourage the coins to slide down the chute as they plop one after another into the hungry box.

Medical services

Each of our four cities has well-organised international clinics, open 24 hours a day and staffed with medical teams who can speak English and other languages.

If you are sick, ask your Rep or hotel reception to call a doctor; or, if possible, go to a clinic direct. Surgeries can be identified by a red cross on a white background. The usual cost is 4,000 ptas a visit, which you pay yourself. Remember to keep any doctor or chemist receipts, to back whatever insurance claim you may have.

Chemists – Farmacias – are marked by a green cross. There's always a night-duty chemist in each city district, and the rota is posted on the door of any pharmacy. Otherwise, consult 'farmacias de guardia' – the duty pharmacists – in the daily paper for addresses.

WC guidance

Public Toilets: Don't waste time trying to find any! Use a café or bar, leaving a token tip if you're not drinking or buying anything. In the newer establishments, you can open the appropriate door – Señoras or Caballeros – with optimism.

Otherwise, in side-street bars that have seen better days, the arrangements often have a museumpiece atmosphere, very ethnic with a hole in the floor. Other facilities may be lacking. Sometimes the gap between utter misery and fulfillment is measured by a few sheets of toilet paper. Always carry a small supply in your holdall, in case of desperate emergency.

News

UK morning newspapers arrive by afternoon in Madrid and Barcelona, somewhat later in Seville, and next day in Granada. Typical newspaper prices are around 200 pesetas for the heavy dailies; 400 pesetas for the posh Sundays; 160 pesetas for the daily tabloids.

Most of the larger hotels are now equipped to receive satellite TV, and can offer 24-hour choice of CNN or Sky News; or MTV, Super Channel, Eurosport or Sky One.

A five-minute summary of ITV News is broadcast Monday to Friday on Spanish TV E2, in the afternoon Tele Europa programme.

If your holiday would be ruined without vital home news like up-to-date Test Match scores, it's worth packing a short-wave radio, to catch the regular on-the-hour news bulletins of the BBC World Service. Best wave-lengths for Spain are:
Early morning – 9410 on 31-meter band; 6195 on 49m band; 7185 on 41m band.
Daytime – 12095 on 25-meter band; 15070 on 19m band.
Evening – 12095 on 25-meter band; 9410 on 31m band; 6195 on 49m band.

Reception varies greatly according to time and location. Reception can be greatly improved with an external aerial. A length of wire dangling over your balcony can make all the difference. Medium or long wave cannot be relied upon, but you could always try your luck on 639 or 648.

Public Holidays

On public holidays, all shops, banks and travel agencies are closed. Museums are mostly open with Sunday timings.
Jan 1 – New Year's Day; Jan 6 – Ephiphany; Good Friday; Easter Monday; May 1 – May Day; mid-May – Pentecost; June 24 – St. John's Day (Barcelona); Aug 15 – Day of the Assumption; Sep 11 – 'La Diada' national festivities of Catalonia; Oct 12 – Day of the Spanish Speaking Nations; Nov 1 – All Saints' Day; Dec 6 – Constitution Day; Dec 8 – the Immaculate Conception; Dec 25/26 – Christmas.

More information

Addresses in Britain

Spanish National Tourist Office, 57/58 St. James's Street, London SW1A 1LD. Tel: 0171-499 0901. Fax: 0171-629 4257. Open Mon-Fri 9-17 hrs.

Spanish Consulate General, 20 Draycott Place, London SW3 2RZ. Tel: 0171-581 5921/6. Fax: 0171-581 7888. Open Mon-Fri 9.30–14.30 hrs. Closed October 12 and all British public holidays.

INFORMATION

Iberia: Venture House, 29 Glasshouse Street, London W1R 5RG. Tel: 0171-437 5622 Reservations (open 9.00–18.00 hrs). Tel: 0171-830 0011 Flight Enquiries. Fax: 0171-434 3375.

Iberia also operates regional offices in Aberdeen, Belfast, Birmingham, Bournemouth, Bristol, Cardiff, Douglas – Isle of Man, Dublin, Edinburgh, Glasgow, Leeds/Bradford, Liverpool, London-Heathrow, Manchester Airport, Newcastle and Nottingham.

Addresses in North America

Tourist Office of Spain:
665 Fifth Ave, New York 10022. Tel: 759 8822.
845 North Michigan Ave, Water Tower Place, Suite 915 East, Chicago, Ill 60611. Tel: 944 0216
8383 Wilshire Blvd, Suite 960, Beverly Hills, CA 90211. Tel: 658 7188.
1221 Brickell Ave., Miami, FL 33131. Tel: 358 1992.
102 Bloor Street West, 14th Floor, Toronto, Ontario M5S 1M8. Tel: 961 3131.

Spanish Embassy: 2700 15th St NW, Washington DC 2009. Tel: 265 0190.

Spanish Consulates:
150 East 58th St, 16th Floor, New York 10155. Tel: 355 4080.
Other consulates are located in Boston, Chicago, Houston, Los Angeles, Miami, New Orleans, San Francisco and Washington DC.

Iberia:
97-77 Queens Blvd., Rego Park, New York 11374 for Information – Tel: 793 3300.
565 Fifth Ave, New York 10017 – Tel: 309 8766.

Emergency telephone number
Police 091